The BAFFLER

Number Ten

9

D1508955

Thomas Frank, editor-in-chief
Greg Lane, publisher
Matt Weiland, managing editor
David "Diamonds" Mulcahey, Keith White, senior editors
Maura Mahoney, Tom Vanderbilt, associates
Damon Krukowski, Jennifer Moxley, poetry

The Baffler wishes to thank George Hodak and Jim McNeill for Hodakizing this number, Nelson Lichtenstein, Mark Crispin Miller, Lewis Lapham, Elaine Bernard, Peter Rachleff, and Robert McChesney for helping with our Fall 1997 book tour, Tom Holert of *Spex* for assistance beyond the call of duty, and Kirstin Peterson and her colleagues for trans-disciplinary advice. We would also especially like to thank 57th Street Books, St. Marks Books, Rainbow Bookstore, Hungry Mind Bookstore, Shaman Drum Bookshop, and Powell's Books.

Please note that The Baffler is, yes, *still* an independent magazine. It's not owned by anybody, unless you count its editors. Keep your eyes open for *Commodify Your Dissent* (Norton), an anthology of essays from old Bafflers (which is basically the only way you're going to find that stuff, since almost no libraries subscribed back then), *The Conquest of Cool* (University of Chicago Press), Tom Frank's book on what a great time we had in the sixties, and *Notes from Underground* (Verso), Steve Duncombe's book on what a great time we are having now.

Baffler office-pest Owen Hatteras is building a collection of commodified-deviance Americana. Whenever you come across an ad for a furniture store peddling revolution, or a brand of jeans called "chaos," tell him about it. He can be reached c/o The Baffler.

Check it out! For a limited time, you can buy copies of Baffler #9, the labor issue, for $10. Otherwise, subscriptions are $20 for four issues; $36 for eight. There are no writers' guidelines at The Baffler. Except for poets: We no longer accept unsolicited poetry. Sorry.

Direct everything else to us at
P. O. Box 378293, Chicago, IL 60637

Babbitt Rex

Boob and Boho in the Businessman's Republic

THOMAS FRANK

If you can't beat 'em, join 'em, goes the native adage; but in the case of [Sinclair] Lewis and America, it is difficult to say who joined up with whom.

—*Steven Marcus, 1963*

THE Cartesians of this world must find it difficult to listen to WYPA, the Chicago AM radio station that fills its broadcast schedule with a torrent of three- and four-minute talks on aspects of success, leadership, and entrepreneurial virtue. Not only does the object of desire shift maddeningly from minute to minute—achievement, goals, "conversation power," the ability to read, big houses, social success for the kiddies—but each of the day's thirty or forty lecturers suggests a different protocol or lifelong regimen for attaining whatever it is, usually something involving numerology or alliteration. There's the "friendly, fair, and flexible" system; there's the fellow who has discovered that the way to go through life is to "match and mirror" other people's gestures, inflections, expressions, and accents. Another exhorts listeners to acquire "the habit of visualization," to run an "instant pre-play" of everything we say and do. A fourth instructs us to impose order on our lives by writing a "personal mission statement," just as the Founding Fathers are said to have done with the Constitution, "the standard of excellence for the land." Inspirers pause in mid-sentence to spell out an acronym for the word they have just uttered, revealing what each letter stands for (". . . smart. The acronym is: Successful, Manageable, Attainable, Realistic, and Trackable.") as though it were the most natural thing in the world, the way Adam or Shakespeare or Webster thought them all up in the first place. Then there are the zanier exhortations which understand business endeavor as a transcendental state, a quest for oceanic oneness with the timeless spirit of acquisition: Last summer the easy winner in this category was the trippy gospel of "Flow," which counsels all manner of marketing managers and photocopier salesmen on the virtues of "becoming immersed," getting "in-groove," and "learning to enjoy the immediate experience."

To listen to "Personal Achievement Radio" for the first time is a thrilling experience. Here, it seems, is the last frontier of virgin, unironized kitsch: cheesy soundtracks and tinny voice-overs, transparent hucksterism and pathetic sincerity, all emanating from the low end of the AM—*AM!*—dial.

The feeling of bottomless banality is heightened by the peppy patter of the DJs, who introduce each mini-sermon as though inspiration was just as interchangeable as Top-40 music, with Zig Ziglar in the place of, say, Ace of Base. But however sedulously the various stars of WYPA may have embraced current buzzwords (one boosts a Web site publishing only good news), there's an unmistakable echo in their routines of the business patter Sinclair Lewis satirized in his 1922 novel, *Babbitt*. Sometimes the resemblance is so exact that one might well be listening to a radio station whose signals have been bouncing around the Solar System since the days of Coolidge. Consider this passage from *Babbitt*, a statement of principle given by one of Zenith's leading advertising men at a meeting of the city's Boosters' Club, but which could easily (with only a few words changed) enliven the afternoon rotation on WYPA:

> Service finds its broadest opportunity and development only in its broadest and deepest application and the consideration of its perpetual action upon reaction. I believe the highest type of Service, like the most progressive tenets of ethics, senses unceasingly and is motived by active adherence and loyalty to that which is the essential principle of Boosterism—Good Citizenship in all its factors and aspects.

From the crude days of One Hundred Percent Pep and Dale Carnegie down to the sophisticated postmodern transcendentalism of Flow, this hollow gospel of affirmation has been the public mythology of our economic order, relentlessly turning any questions about larger purpose back on the individual, casting any society-wide failings as symptoms of your personal failure to be sufficiently affirmative. While it may be pitiable in its obvious meretriciousness, its sham scholarship, its desperately repeated assurances that the pixies of success will someday promote each of us to "executive" status, it is also the folklore of power, the catechism of our national faith. Like George F. Babbitt, the average WYPA listener is hardly a great titan of business, but it is nonetheless appropriate to apply to him, in his mountainous will to believe, Sinclair Lewis's reference to his subject as "the ruler of America . . . . Our conqueror, dictator over our commerce, education, labor, art, politics, morals, and lack of conversation."

Seventy-five years later, as the free-market faith stands on the verge of becoming a national cult, as superstar entrepreneurs and the power of positive thinking become objects of both journalistic reverence and cinematic homage, *Babbitt* appears like a manifesto of American satire, a model for the sound thrashing so richly deserved by all our contemporary priests of boosterism. Even today Lewis's cast of characters are still easily recognizable as contemporary types: the authoritative economist, the charlatan business school professor, the lyricist of the American salesman who writes advertising on the side.

Lewis's description of the some-times bizarre minutiae of middle-class life is similarly enduring: the story of the man who lords his low license plate number over his colleagues at the Elks; the realtors singing Zenith's official city song on their way to the convention; the characters marvelling over the comical slang of the newspaper advertisements. Each could have happened yesterday.

But *Babbitt* is also a strangely limited satire, easy even for those who inhabit the same social and regional place as George F. Babbitt to regard as a document strictly of its time, a painstaking description of life in a particular social stratum in the American Midwest in 1922. Despite some surface similarities, the Midwestern cities that Zenith has grown into don't really suffocate people in the blunt and obtuse way Sinclair Lewis described. One can even read *Babbitt* as a sort of cultural analog of Upton Sinclair's *The Jungle*, a critique which served its purpose at the time but which progress has superseded. This is at least partially attributable to Lewis's powers of literary demolition: For at least ten years his scorn was capable of obsoleting entire bodies of slang, style, and belief; his drolleries became overnight buzzwords and universal epithets.

Which raises the most interesting aspect of *Babbitt* at 75: the dynamic relationship between *Babbitt* and the Babbittry—what we might call the *Babbitt* Equation. Babbitts coast to coast bought the book in huge numbers; the newspapers of any number of Midwestern cities

insisted that *their* burg was his model for Zenith; and legions of individuals claimed to be Babbitt himself. The book does not include a chapter in which George F. Babbitt sails into a Zenith book shop and picks up a novel savaging his fellow boosters, but it might well have done so. The real lesson of *Babbitt*, it turned out, was that smug self-satisfaction thrives in a strange symbiosis with self-loathing in the soul of the American businessman, the two driving him to acts that look simultaneously like bold self-overcoming and a dog chasing its tail. What *Babbitt* revealed was that the American business class enjoys few things more than a witty dressing-down of just this type, the author's sympathy for the regular guys showing clearly through his good-natured mockery.

Consider the specific criticism of business civilization that the book makes. George F. Babbitt may be successful but he is a boor, a man who has turned his back on true feeling and filled his life with emotion-substitutes, with empty talk of zest and zip. The guy even sells suburban homes for a living! The commercial imperatives that dominate his world are fake, hollow, and tasteless. This is a point that Lewis wanted to be sure nobody misunderstood, driving it home dogmatically in the maudlin story of Babbitt's artist-manqué friend Paul Riesling (he who sighs at a steel mill's "picturesque" beauty) and in the unspoken admissions of Babbitt himself that "his way of life [was] incredibly mechanical."

Again and again, Lewis has Babbitt and his fellow Zip Citians encounter bits of the real high culture stuff (Dante, Virgil, the classical columns in the movie theater, a "marble seat warm from five hundred summers of Amalfi"), and follows each meeting invariably and automatically with some act of degradation or some incomprehensible crassitude. The reader's response was no doubt meant to be equally invariable and automatic: We cluck disapprovingly, shake our head over the illiteracy of these boobs, and realize that the great tragedy of middle-class life is its distance from the sacred stuff of culture. When Lewis gives us passages like the hilariously banal newspaper poetry of Chum Frink (which, guess what, actually celebrates conformity and cultural standardization) or records Babbitt's proud declaration that "in America the successful writer or picture-painter is indistinguishable from any other decent business man," he is setting up one of the criticisms of American life that he would later make explicit in his Nobel acceptance speech. While we Americans had proven our ability to amass capital proper, we were sadly deficient in acquiring cultural capital, the real stuff of social class.

This rather predictable line of criticism makes up one side of the *Babbitt* Equation: The businessman as boob. So easy a critique is it that *Babbitt*'s understanding of business life itself quickly became a standard element of business life, just one more item on the long list of self-improvements that we resolve to make as part of Philistine No Longer! or the Ten Days to Wit and Culture system.

The urgent cultural struggle of 1922 was the overthrow of the "genteel tradition" in American letters, the destruction of what H. L. Mencken called "puritanism as a literary force." The enthusiastic public reception of *Babbitt* marked both the victory of the scoffers and the beginning of a great shift in the cultural battleground. What is remembered less clearly is how Lewis's attack on the boorish tastes and unfulfilling life of the bourgeoisie fit the old puritan agenda, especially its tendency toward introspection and self-condemnation. Lewis didn't renounce middle-class life (as did John Dos Passos and Floyd Dell) so much as call for a slight alteration of its goals. In *Babbitt* we can glimpse the first flashes of a new but still unmistakably middle-class style, what we might call bourgeois self-loathing as a literary force. Whether Lewis's own name is remembered twenty years from now or not (and the steady downward trajectory of his fame suggests the latter), he created in 1922 a straw man of archetypal durability whose tepid tastes and insensitivity to culture will draw the hoots of the complacent middle class for decades to come. And for the left politics in which Lewis ached to participate, *Babbitt* substituted a politics of authenticity, an aestheticized struggle still fought today through TV commercials and in the lyrics of an army of lavishly alienated tattoo boys.

So while WYPA and its thick fog of patriotic positivity hold down one side of the *Babbitt* Equation, the other becomes more ubiquitous with every passing year, as $Babbitt_2$ screams to the world that he's *not* a "Standardized American Citizen." Today $Babbitt_2$ frequents fashionable restaurants and offers loud disquisitions on Midwesterners' lamentable taste for iceberg lettuce, on their full and total ignorance of radicchio; $Babbitt_2$ reads *The New Yorker*, where mildly daring slaps at middle-class propriety bracket fawning accounts of the captains of industry; $Babbitt_2$ reveres not bland Rotarians but the extreme executives whose mad flava is detailed month after month in the business press. But for a truly candid picture of the two Babbitts locked in sham battle with each other, just move your tuner to an NPR affiliate for a few hours. One day recently the network presented a lengthy management jeremiad given by a leading CEO and followed it, immediately and quite unproblematically, with an inside look at the Tejano poetry scene, a gorgeously untouched backcountry bohemia where people are still in touch with the natural order, authenticity can be found at every backyard barbecue, nobody has been corrupted by the ways of the big city, and everyone seems to suffer from the curious delusion that they are fine poets.

Of course, what makes *Babbitt* a truly great satire is the fact that Lewis seemed to know that he was setting up a largely bogus opposition. Consider, for example, the episode four-fifths of the way through the book in which George F. Babbitt suddenly declares himself "in rebellion" and takes up with a crowd of Zenith bohemians. Many critics have taken exception to this plot turn, finding a fatal inconsistency in Babbitt's overnight change from iron complacency into nonconformity. But how different are the two Babbitts really? Contemporary readers find nothing odd about the idea of a realtor doing a little subcultural dabbling on the side—today it's virtually a part of the job, a mandatory prerequisite for anyone looking to do some speculation in the next hot neighborhood. It seems obvious now that Babbitt as a consorter with tippling aesthetes is still Babbitt the real-estate manipulator; that bohemia is just as much a boob's game as is selling prefab houses in Floral Heights.

So thoroughly are all the Babbittry "in rebellion" today, of course, that the literary anniversary for which they boost with punch and pep is not the seventy-fifth of *Babbitt* but the fortieth of *On the Road*, an installment in the literature of bourgeois self-loathing so aesthetically predictable that it might better be titled *Son of Babbitt*. By 1957, though, the requirements had changed. Nobody wanted to read more details of middle-class life, so Kerouac cut the criticism, focused exclusively on the shallow soul-searching and boho merry-making, and thereby hit upon the formula that, even today, brings the people of Zenith back to the bookstores, the cineplexes, the TV sets. Forget the fine points of business civilization, the mundane idiocies; what the fellow on Main Street wants to hear about is exotic enlightenment, Benzedrine tubes, big chunks of authentic dharma, the car-stuff. So while the seventy-fifth anniversary of Sinclair Lewis's masterpiece is marked with paperback editions by small presses, *On the Road* is reissued as a hardbound by Viking and continues to sell (according to a recent report in the *New York Times Magazine*) more than a hundred thousand copies a year. Still, Kerouac's indebtedness to Lewis is such that *On the Road* could well be read as one long homage to the advertisement for Zeeco cars that Chum Frink, the poet, recites at Babbitt's dinner party:

> The long white trail is calling—calling—and it's over the hills and far away for every man or woman that has red blood in his veins and on his lips the ancient song of the buccaneers. It's away with dull drudging, and a fig for care. Speed—glorious Speed—it's more than just a moment's exhilaration—it's Life for you and me! . . . . Listen, brother! You'll never know what the high art of hiking is till you TRY LIFE'S ZIPPINGEST ZEST—THE ZEECO!

Allons Enfants de la Zip Cit-ee

ONE can only marvel at the devastation a satirist like Lewis could wreak in this age of overwrought free-market proclamations, of corporate millennialism and Wall Street astrology. Radicchio and Jack Kerouac notwithstanding, Babbitt seems to have become "ruler," "conqueror," and "dictator" not only over American "commerce, education, labor, art, politics, morals," but over the world's.

Almost exactly 75 years to the day after *Babbitt* appeared, the *International Herald Tribune* offered as its lead European headline a rosy "New Credo for [the] World." The story's first sentence, penned by Barbara Crossette of the *New York Times*, rivals—even mimics—the gushing phrases of advertising in its transcendent optimism: "Has there ever been a moment quite like this?" Back in America, Crossette announces with the smug confidence of a speaker at a Rotary Club luncheon, the class problem has been largely solved, as "high-yield retirement accounts are making near-millionaires of thousands of salaried workers and hourly wage earners." Elsewhere in the world, she asserts, ancient conflicts are also disappearing under the benevolent pressure of sound business practices. Crossette is merely trying her hand at this year's big journalistic idea, of course, and her effort is distinguished only by the fact that she dispenses with caution and humility more recklessly than last week's entry in the *Financial Times* or wherever. The barrage continues in an article slightly lower on the page which carefully excepts the sneering French from this worldwide society of Solid Citizens and Regular Fellows. France's mulish insistence on maintaining a welfare state and its arrogant repudiation of American leadership have made it, from here to *The New Republic*, the editorialist's favorite target, the French now the inevitable cranks and knockers to the responsible journalist's vision of Progress, Prosperity, and One-Hundred-Per-Cent Pep.

Crossette is a lesser pom-pom on the American free-market cheerleading squad that stars Robert Samuelson, Thomas Friedman, and Charles Krauthammer. And while their writing may consist largely of twentieth-generation repetitions of the stuff that makes up Babbitt's speech to the Zenith Boosters' Club, lately their ambitions have been anything but provincial. In this age of Clinton the American pundits have seen the old boundaries of taste, humility, and nation-states give way before them, and with an almost supernatural force the conviction has dawned on them that the American booster's way of life can be—*must be!*—extended to the rest of the planet.

But can we all become Babbitt? The repeated journalistic attacks on the French for their alleged refusal to welcome market principles—attacks that always equate the French welfare state with snobbery—inevitably call to mind the first part of the *Babbitt* Equation: bourgeois as boob, market man as proud philistine. It can't be long before the *Wall Street Journal* announces that the world

A Question of Size

Doug Henwood

Everybody loves small business. Politicians use plucky little enterprises as the cover for schemes to cut taxes and ease regulations for their Fortune 500 constituencies. Pundits assure us that small business is a fount of jobs and innovation, a hotbed of entrepreneurship led by iconoclasts who thrive on making life difficult for sclerotic megacorporate bureaucracies. Tininess has earned additional press in recent years, as the network model of business organization—weightless decentralized units linked by fiber optics—is celebrated in business journals and MCI ads. Even postmodernish greens, no friends of business, celebrate the small variety as localist, friendly, and sensitive—not cold and alienating like the global behemoths.

Almost none of which is accurate. Small business creates jobs, yes, but it also destroys them in large numbers, since small firms go under so frequently. Small business pays less, innovates less, invests less, and probably does more physical damage to nature and workers than the big guys. There may be social or aesthetic reasons to prefer small firms—informality, face-to-faceness, whatever—but their much-heralded economic virtues don't survive scrutiny.

The political prestige of small business comes from the widely circulated but untrue "fact" that it's the source of 80 percent of the new jobs in America. This factoid can be traced to work done by a consultant, one David Birch of Cognetics Inc., who analyzed some computer tapes from the credit rating and business information firm Dun & Bradstreet in a report he did for the Commerce Department in 1979. From there the factoid ascended into soundbite fame in the eighties and early nineties. Other researchers also used the D&B data, and even the U.S. Small Business Administration did for a while too. But a closer examination conducted some years later showed the D&B tapes to be full of errors, at odds not only with official unemployment insurance registration info, but even with the phone book. And Birch's methodology was pretty idiosyncratic, to put it kindly. One particularly goofy example: The Small Business Administration defines a small firm as one with fewer than 500 employees. In Birch's rendering of the D&B data, if a firm with 600 employees had a bad year and canned 200 of them, this would show up as a gain of 400 jobs for the small business sector! Other enthusiastic studies count job growth, but forget job loss when putting the numbers together. Strangely, these devastating discoveries—outlined by Dan Cordtz in the April 26, 1994, issue of **Financial World**—have caused not even the slightest downturn in the ideological prestige of small business.

More rigorous work, like that done for the U.S. Census Bureau based on its industrial surveys and that by New School economist Bennett Harrison, shows that there's absolutely no relation between firm size and the propensity to create jobs. The same with age: Startups may be glamorous, but they are also the most likely to crash and burn.

What about the other virtues of small

will live under the specter of snob and socialist until AM transmitters broadcasting the purest principles of positivity are set up from Biarritz to Bourges; until the transcendent peace of Flow is made available to Communist charwomen and hairsplitting academics from Calais to Cannes.

Yet the Chum Frinks of the American media have little to worry about. The evening that Crossette's proud boasts crossed the cover of the *Herald Tribune* I went to dinner with six businesspeople, all young, well-educated, and cosmopolitan: one British, one Italian, one Swiss, one Dutch, one American, and one French. The conversation moved through topics that any reader of Pierre Bourdieu's 1979 book, *Distinction*, could easily have predicted: questions of art, architecture, and history that always seem to interest members of the new managerial class. No one was embarrassed or silenced by ignorance; no one bleated crudely in the Babbitt manner; the American was not ugly. Then someone mentioned Tom Peters, and the table erupted with loud disquisitions on this or that theme in the great consultant's work. Everyone had read him—*they'd read every book he's written*—and they had each internalized his advice, embraced his thoughts on human enterprise as though Peters personally had stood over their shoulder and interpreted his athletic prose for them. An argument grew over whether Peters' latest books, the hopelessly commercial paperbacks *Pursuit of Wow* and *Crazy Times Call for Crazy Organizations*, were or were not a betrayal of the weighty thoughts of earlier works like *Thriving on Chaos*. It was agreed, though, that Peters' meditations on "excellence" rank among the century's most significant thinkings; that his contribution to that body of theory we call management tower above all others.

Look in the right places and the creeping Babbittization of Europe starts to resemble one of the thousand paranoid subplots of a Pynchon novel, evidence of some grand scheme cropping up everywhere. One spots a copy of *Getting to Yes* on the bedside table of an otherwise hardheaded young Dutch foreign trade analyst; one listens as a rising Italian real-estate developer, after fairly literate talk about that nation's class system and his experiences in the Vatican library, confides earnestly that one must (a) understand productive life as a journey and

(b) learn the universal principles of Flow. Not that anyone here seems to have any more of an idea what this stuff means than the listeners of WYPA; American management talk is revered nonetheless, taken as a sort of totem—a status made possible by its very meaninglessness—of inexplicable prosperity.

The other side of the *Babbitt* Equation, the fake opposition, is almost impossible to miss in Western Europe, but here all of Lewis's categories of reverence for European culture-stuff have been nicely inverted. Again "America" is understood mystically, but here it is U.S. junk culture that is revered, taken as a totem of the freedom available in Kerouac-kountry, the United States as a theme park of authenticity and unaffected expression, as a refuge from the Old World grind. If the omnipresent MTV knock-offs and anglophone Scandinavian pop bands aren't enough, take the mad fantasies of American authenticity, American commercial practices (both honest and lazy), and nose-thumbing American disobedience (never disobedient enough to stage a general strike or secure a national health care plan) posited by the faux-American T-shirt slogans so popular among French, Spanish, Belgian, Dutch, and German vacationers (all spotted within the space of one hour on the beach at a popular French resort town):

"Wild Reserve"

"Back to my Roots"

"Original Grade"

"Biscuit Clothing: For Something Original"

"Ethnic West Coast Revolution"

"Wear the Blue: Our Style Remain"

"No Work Team" (fairly ubiquitous on T-shirts, bumper stickers, and surfboards)

"Street Te@m"

"Local Boyz Quality Trademark"

and, on a scooter, a slogan that would have made Babbitt proud: "Booster Spirit."

We Are All Sinclair Lewis Now

At the downtown campus of the University of Chicago Graduate School of Business the contrast between neighborhood residents and students is not quite as remarkable as it is on the main South Side cam-

business—say, innovation? Sometimes new firms do create new industries—like DEC in minicomputers or Apple in PCs (neither of which is thriving in 1997)—but after a while, big firms that innovate through organized industrial research take over the new industry. This is because big firms have a big productivity edge. They have capital to spend, huge economies of scale, and a financial cushion sufficient to absorb failures. This is not just true of individual firms: Whole industrial sectors dominated by big firms also have the best productivity numbers. In **Creating the Computer**, Kenneth Flamm demonstrates that IBM's market dominance in the fifties and sixties enabled it to fund R&D that would have been beyond the capacity of firms earning lower competitive rates of profit.

Of course, one could argue that innovation isn't all it's cracked up to be, and that much of it is designed to increase profit and stimulate sales rather than improve human welfare. One could also argue that the production of more stuff more cheaply isn't really all that winning a basis for a civilization. But regardless of where you stand on such fundamental questions, one ought to be clear on which part of the economy does what.

The facts, unfortunately, speak for themselves. Big business pays a lot better than small, has a better record of hiring people other than white guys and is more likely to be unionized. In 1994, just 35 percent of workers toiling for bosses with fewer than 100 employees had health insurance, and 19 percent had a pension plan—compared with 68 percent and 62 percent of workers at employers (including governments) with more than 1,000 employees.

But those bigger enterprises employed just 38 percent of the workforce, compared with 43 percent for the smaller. If you take away government workers, just 13 percent of private sector employees work at firms where they have 1,000 or more colleagues. If you ascend the scale of grandness to the Fortune 500, you're talking about even fewer workers.

One way to think about the U.S. economy might be this: Giant businesses, which employ only a fraction of the labor force, are so monstrously productive that we all live off their crumbs. Their high-paid employees produce the cheap light bulbs and expensive CAT scanners that make industrial life possible, and provide the supplier contracts that keep smaller firms going. They also buy and sell politicians, fund think tanks, and make advertising—in other words, they (try to) tell us how to think and feel.

Maybe official celebrations of small business should be seen in another light—as a more or less open admission of the owning classes' desires to cut pay and slash benefits. Whatever the facts about small business, the U.S. economy shows lower levels of real investment and productivity growth than its peers, plus dismal wage performance. What the U. S. economy does best is keep lots of low-paid workers in low-productivity service jobs, just the kind small businesses excel at providing. Why most of us are supposed to be happy about this situation is anyone's guess. But to the American elite, there is no mystery—it's wonderful for stock and bond prices, and isn't that the real test?

pus. But still the kids are something to see as they come rolling up to the shiny new North Loop complex in taxis and company-provided limos: the designated captains of whatever industry will still be left twenty years from now, the most promising junior executives in the world, hailing from all corners of the globe but still admirably uniform in thought, expression, clothing, and bearing; a homogeneous transnational business class, in straight teeth and standard-issue Burberry, stationed here in Babbitt country for a few years to soak up the timeless principles of Vision, Ideals, Inspiration, and, well, Pep. Tonight the tag-team scholars in charge, postmodern thinkers who celebrate what they call "non-linear thinking" and the transdisciplinary principles of Flow, have arranged for this golden throng a lecture by a marketplace thaumaturge of the thousand-percent variety, a bona fide *artist* whose talk leads the prodigies of the future directly into their first assignment: comparing the creativity and transgressiveness of Jasper Johns and Warren Buffett. Then it's on to part two, the Sinclair Lewis exercise, in which the students are asked to invent personifications of two corporate organizations, one effervescently entrepreneurial, the other supported by (ugh!) state subsidies. To a man, the students have opted to cast the upstart firm as an outsider artist of some kind, the daughter of a Jamaican mother and an Italian father, a painter, a singer, an aficionado of sports and e-communication and exotic travel. The decrepit old company, meanwhile, is said to be a corpulent, tired, middle-aged, and distinctly white male beneficiary of some kind of nepotism—it's George F. Babbitt.

One professor tells the proto-executives about the weighty yet glorious burden of "vision," about how it sometimes puts one at odds with the little people, the mundanely details-oriented. He reads from *Leadership Without Easy Answers*. He informs them that vision is a "spiritual" quality, while "mission" is more of a "left-brain" function. He lists the "Three Enabling Forces." He tells them about "Personal Meaning." And after a taped speech by the late Leo Burnett on the nature of creativity, he dismisses the students back into the night, to the taxis and company-provided limos, off to ponder, with the glamorous sense of responsibility peculiar to those born to power, the pleasantly arduous future stretching out ahead; all the boardroom battles with all the right-brained Babbitts of the older generation that lie before them, and that they are certain to win. What they have listened to for the last three hours, of course, is only marginally more useful than what they could have learned from a day's close attention to "Personal Achievement Radio" or a volume by Napoleon Hill. But that's not the point: Corporate bohemianism may be intellectually vacuous, but it works for them like the Great Chain of Being worked for medieval kings, a sound and convincing lesson in class entitlement, in the rightness and justness of the world, and in their own place in it.

Of course, to understand these golden avatars of creative corporate practice as largely identical to the boorish, slow-moving executives they believe to be their forebears, is to commit what they would no doubt regard as an act of inexcusable intellectual insensitivity. And as the republic of business extends its benevolent shade over the globe, the minor differences between the Elks Club variant of Babbitt and his China Club cousin— like the distance between radicchio and iceberg or between Bill Clinton and Bob Dole— will expand with it, until that fine day when the *Babbitt* Equation, the imaginary war of boob and boho, ingenue and ironist, philistine and connoisseur, will be the only public choice we have left.

For beneath the banal patter of the Babbittry is a public philosophy as comprehensive and as capable of explaining the world as any mankind has ever devised, one that works for those on the bottom as well as for those on top. I recall an enthusiastic young man who attended an institution of management training where they skipped the fine points about Jasper Johns and studied the rudiments of salesmanship instead. Still the curriculum amounted to pretty much the same thing—round upon round of hollow positivity-talk. But for my friend its promise was just as defi-

Attitude
<u>Pre</u>-tested
before a dime
is Invested

nite as it is for the gilded Babbitts$_2$ of Chicago: This was to be his escape from the dull West Virginia wastes in which he had been reared; the way into a world of luxury and firm handshakes and masculine bonhomie that he was capable of imagining as vividly as any Dreiser character, and into the attainment of which he threw himself blindly and wholeheartedly. He understood the job offer he received just before graduation as the long-awaited summons into the executive class of his dreams, and he promptly betook himself to the Pontiac dealership in our university town and purchased a brand new Trans-Am.

The junior executives made short work of him, of course, finding in his eagerly gaping face an irresistible target. Over the years he bounced from firm to firm, the enthusiasm that made him so vulnerable dimming with each disaster, and today he passes his hours in a cubicle near a cloverleaf, cold-calling. Between calls he flips compulsively through a pack of flashcards inscribed with phrases like "I am a successful individual," messages of full-strength, max-volume positivity, stripped of subtlety and undiluted by adverbs, 120-proof reassurance for one whose desperation has become intolerable.

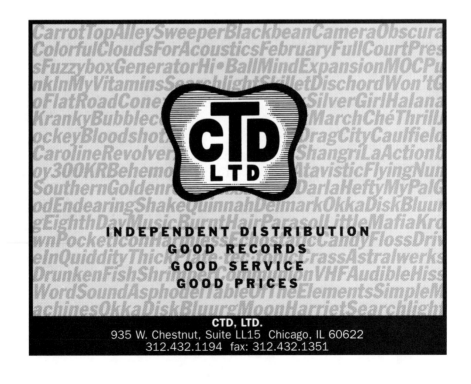

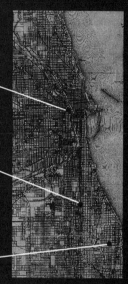

THE GAUDY AND DAMNED
Tom Vanderbilt

F every society makes myths to explain the great and unknowable forces of the world, the age of advanced consumer capitalism has wrought its own peculiar mythology: the brand. What originated as a means of selling standardized products across a mass market—essentially eliminating the need for the salesman—has evolved into a hybrid religion, social system, philosophy, and, finally, way of life. The swooshes and arches that dot our landscape and adorn our apparel are sacred symbols imparting, according to certain marketers, a "halo effect" on their purchasers. Things that are not products at all—art museums, university educations, film studios—are subsumed by branded thought (a recent book called *Scotland: The Brand* gets at the heart of this); and brands become a sort of personality extension providing an appropriate product for each part of the lifestyle to which you have subscribed.

In a recent issue of *Fast Company*, Tom Peters ("the world's leading brand when it comes to writing, speaking, or thinking about the new economy") suggests that the relationship between people and brands

be taken to its next logical step: "The Brand Called You." For Peters, this "new brand world," in which people compose identities through logos on their shoes or their coffee cups, provides valuable lessons for corporate power brokers trying to move up in a career world characterized more by lilypads than ladders. Peters, with his logo-centric worldview, is a conspiracy theorist of brands: He seems to see them everywhere. We visit Web sites because "the brand name tells you that the visit will be worth your time"; when you sift through your e-mail messages, deleting some and answering others, you're responding to the "brands" you like and receiving a "promise of the value you'll receive for the time you spend reading the message." The language of the marketplace, in other words, can be used to describe the most personal human interactions. Everything, Peters is here to tell us, can be reduced to the level of a saleable commodity.

Peters would sound crazier were brands not exerting such a tremendous pull on contemporary society. There is nothing new about brand loyalty, of course, but in recent

years it has acquired a certain devotional tinge, evolving into a virtual belief system—accompanied by our ever-expanding consumer tithe. The brand becomes, in the words of one marketer, "a story that's evolving all the time," thereby justifying both constant obsolescence and endless product "extensions," in which all manner of spin-offs take their place in the drama. Brand theaters like the Viacom Entertainment Center and Nike Town are built to facilitate the show. And the story, increasingly, is what we purchase: It's hard to imagine someone entering a Warner Bros. store with an actual product in mind. Nowadays brands actually outgrow products: Nike, Fila, and Reebok, for example, have seen sales of branded apparel grow more quickly than shoes over the past several years (for Nike, apparel now represents nearly half of its domestic profits).

What is ironic about brands as narratives is that they serve to con-

ceal a vast network of economic arrangements and human labor that the buyer never sees. For a brand to become really important the original "story" of a product must have stopped making sense; Starbucks once may have relied on word of mouth to lure customers to its first Seattle stores, but to bring patrons into suburban strip malls across the country a different story must be created, a story that uses "Seattle" as a shadowy token of something authentic and turns coffee drinking into a fetishized art form, something with which the consumer must have a relationship. As a Starbucks exec said approvingly of Ralph Lauren: "He's not selling saddles. He's using the saddle to tell a story." The tale grows fantastically complex as everything from fragrances to house paints are folded into the plot line.

Even so, Peters's "Brand Called You" marks a dramatic extension of the brand story. While the megamergers and best-selling authors and "all the frenzy at the humongous end of the size spectrum" garner all the attention, Peters confides, the "real action is at the other end. The main chance is becoming a free agent in an economy of free agents, looking to have the best season you can imagine in your field, looking to do your best work and chalk up a remarkable track record, and looking to establish your own microequivalent of the Nike swoosh."

Peters upgrades the old saw "sell yourself" to a fully integrated marketing campaign: "You're every bit as much a brand as Nike, Coke, Pepsi, or The Body Shop," he gushes. The trick is to note what distinguishes you from colleagues, what "feature-benefit model" you offer, and then "market the bejesus" out of Brand You, by moonlighting, writing Op-Eds, creating "braggables," even recruiting a "user's group" to get feedback on your performance. After all, "It's the only way to know what you would be worth on the open market."

In Peters's blustery slew of hyperbole and pseudo-empowerment, common sense masquerades as revelation, facts are preciously thin on the ground, and arguments double back on themselves as just another "boundary" to be quashed, in the same way products "transcend the narrow boundaries of their category and become a brand surrounded by a Tommy Hilfiger-like buzz." The NFL's recent efforts to remake itself as a brand becomes much less remarkable seen from this perspective: Consider how stadiums have become endorsement opportunities, team ownership is now a corporate loss-leader, and top athletes have stronger allegiances (and often larger financial ties) to the companies that sponsor them than to whatever team is currently purchasing their services. It's a "free-agent economy" indeed that governs professional sports, and there must be plenty of admiration in those corporate skyboxes for the personal brands on the playing surface below. Fan loyalty has become perhaps the greatest commodity of all.

As one ad executive for a credit card company was quoted in *The New York Times*, "We want to take the positive equities of the loyal Green Bay fans and try to transfer them over to our Visa brand."

The blind quest for higher profits has done much to undermine loyalty in professional sports, as in companies. For Tom Peters, however, loyalty is more alive than ever. The difference now, says Peters, is that loyalty to one's "projects" or even to "yourself" (can one really be disloyal to one's self?) has replaced "blind loyalty to the company." Let us be clear about what is at stake here. We are, on the one hand, supposed to forget about company loyalty, and on the other, to use brand loyalty to construct our own individuality—by subsuming our individuality into a branded idea of individuality, banking on those things that supposedly set us apart. As we move into the "winner-take-all society," as Robert Frank and Thomas Cook have dubbed it, where a handful of top celebrities, athletes, and executives command the bulk of earnings in any field, Peters's contention that "everyone has a chance to be a brand worthy of remark" sounds like false advertising: Those very brands we are supposed to emulate achieved success by reducing or eliminating the visibility of competing brands. Just as brands mask their origin and the labor that goes into the creating the products behind the logo, Brand You is a nicely individualistic glyph for an age that permits anything but.

SUCCESSITUDES ™

Incenting the extreme professional since 1993

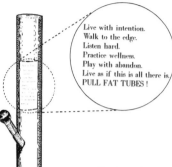

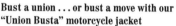

Live with intention.
Walk to the edge.
Listen hard.
Practice wellness.
Play with abandon.
Live as if this is all there is.
PULL FAT TUBES !

The "Pursuit of Wow" bong

Para-sailing at Cabo and snowboarding at Crested Butte may help you to "get to yes," but deep-lung a couple of plumes out of this baby and you'll be at "Fuck yeah!" What executive go-getter wouldn't like to have a hit or two of what Tom Peters has been smoking? 2' plastic Grafix. Red, blue, or green. Brass plaque engraved with inspirational verse of extreme business poet Pringle Pypkin. $129.95.

Bust a union . . . or bust a move with our "Union Busta" motorcycle jacket

Let your restive work force know that you wouldn't think twice about shutting down your box factory and moving it to Arkansas or Mexico. Labor Board approved. Black top-grain leather. $329.95.

Unlock the asshole within . . . with WordBastard™ cassettes

Corporate difference-makers know that the key to extracting peak employee performance is a regime of random and terroristic intimidation. In this nine-tape WordBastard™ set, Dirk Polnschlaeger, the Dean of Executive Intimidation Training, unlocks the secret to life-transforming viciousness. Each day, Dirk will guide you through a series of mental exercises that will teach you the 10 timeless principles of business contumely, the 7 styles of tactical truculence, 6 tips for the up-and-coming martinet, and the 4 qualities of an effective tyrant. The information-packed workbook will hone your skills, and your Personal Bastard Diary will chart your progress. More than a thousand colorful and humiliating commands, imprecations and insults (almost 200 of which refer to the testicles). $89.95.

A Word From Our Chairman

Successitudes™ began with my life-long passion for acquiring stuff — money, cars, fine cigars like this one in my mouth, chicks (of course). I learned long ago that if you want a piece of the action, you gotta strap on a pair of brass ones. Now, some inspirational merchandisers talk a good game about positive mental attitude. They'd have you festoon your office with posters telling you how life is like a golf course and paperweights telling you what T-E-A-M stands for. If that kind of candy-ass uplift makes you feel better about your dead-end middle-management job, fine. But just remember — high-net-worth individuals like myself find chunks of suckers like you in our stools every morning. And that, asshole, is why you should write for our catalog today. P.O. Box 378293, Chicago, IL 60637.

James Hatt

A Partial History of Alarms

NELSON SMITH

THE history of property and theft is a large subject, more or less the history of human-kind. Fully considered, it extends to the bulk of our achievements in government, culture, and commerce, along with the greater share of our technical advances, from the earliest architecture and mightiest engines of war to the humbler topic at hand: electric and electronic security alarms—the various buzzing, shrieking, whooping, clanging, yeeping anti-theft devices so familiar to anyone who lives and sleeps in a modern city.

Though mechanical alarms are fairly recent, the idea is as old as property itself. Undoubtedly, mankind's earliest alarm system consisted of a few strategically tethered dogs. With their jittery, blusterous temperaments and zeal for authority, dogs fully prefigured the basic operating principles of the modern security alarm. Like mechanical alarms—which do not themselves directly attack, roust, or mangle thieves (though such spectacular accessories are now available)—dogs repel intruders with a kind of sonic illusion. Riled, they emit a warning cry in the lowest tone they can muster—a plangent growl whose deep, resonant pitch implies a larger chest, and thus vocal cords attached to a mightier beast. Likewise, security alarms—not in their pitch, but in their broad, systemic reach—imply the attachment of private property to a larger, more brutal entity: the state.

This ventriloquial strategy first took mechanical form in humble alarms for private homes. Before electricity, such devices were relatively feckless, as in the case of an eighteenth-century apparatus of pull-strings and jingle-bells rigged to emit, in the words of its English inventor, "a plaintive air that inspires such sentiments in the mind of the housebreaker that will doubtless prompt him to take precipitous flight."* With electricity, however, plaintiveness became an octave of the alarm's past. According to patent records, the first voltaic "burglar annunciator" was registered in Boston in 1853, making security alarms arguably the earliest form of electrified mass communication. Versions of this novel, window-sprung buzzer were used pri-

---

* From "A History of Alarm Security," by The National Burglar and Fire Alarm Association.

marily to protect the homes of affluent city dwellers. Their jurisdiction was domestic, their advantage surprise. Yet with the technology in place, electric security alarms would soon spread beyond this limited purview in a steady, raucous encroachment of private distress on public domain.

COMMERCIAL alarms marked the next major epoch of alarm development. By the turn of the century, on-premise commercial alarms formed part of the emerging urban network of telegraphs, telephones, pneumatic tubes, fire bells, traffic signals, and other conveyers of modern urgency. Proliferating along the new overhead wireways, a growing alarm industry affixed its clamorous wares to banks, furriers, jewelers, and, above all, to department store windows, where newly fashionable dioramas of mannequins reveling in convenience formed the stroll-by television of the day. Able to reinforce glass without obstructing the view, electric window alarms thus advanced to new heights the technical fusion of display and restriction so essential to the formation of a well-stoked consumer economy. Soon store windows everywhere sported that quaint iconography still visible to any appreciative urban stroller today: badge-shaped decals bearing the Kiwanian-era trademarks of the early alarm manufacturers—a goddess in helmet (Holmes Electric Protection), an eagle volant (Merchant Central), a pony expressman (Wells Fargo Security), a winged griffin (DGA Alarm Systems), a

grenadier in a halo of electric bolts (National Guardsman, Inc.)—depictions of the alarms as a constabulary of stern little genies inhabiting the glass.

With this widening protectorate came a fundamental change in the security alarm's mode of operation. While household alarms were designed primarily to consternate burglars and jangle awake the slumbering homeowner, alarms in the commercial setting required third-party intervention. After business hours, that is, the property owner may be nowhere about, and the alarm must act not merely as a warning signal but as an instrument of makeshift recruitment and random public address. In this evolved capacity, then, the security alarm assumes an implicitly civic function. It appeals, like the clarions or church bells of old, to the sense of duty that undergirds all social order, to those nobler instincts of citizenship, reciprocity, and the commonweal by which we band ourselves into stable, productive nations. Naturally, coercion is involved. Amplified with colossal buzzers, pneumatic sirens, and rapid-fire, wall-bolted gongs, the din of a detonated store alarm blaring, ringing, clanging away in the night forcibly conscripts everyone within earshot into the defense of property that isn't theirs and from which they themselves, let us pause to remember, derive neither profit nor reciprocal protection. All the logic of patriotism is there.

Yet while these peace-rending machines spread rapidly through the commercial realm, their placement remained limited to more or less clear physical bounds. Soon, however, alarm technology would take a decidedly metaphysical turn. By the 1940s, the outsized break-ins of world warfare had inspired the development of a new array of infrared and ultrasonic detectors. Incorporating these advances and hewing to the century's emerging spirit of global surveillance and aerial attack, the simple burglar alarm began to evolve into the more intricate and ethereal "security system." Augmented with electromagnetic sensors, the alarm's trip-circuits could now be beamed through the air rather than puttied or taped to breachable surfaces. This refinement proved especially useful for settings of conditional public access. In banks, museums, and other secular institutions, concealed alarms served to reinforce a sense of gloom-based authority, while half reviving, through a sort of technological animism, the modern public's waning dread of unseen powers.

The hidden security system thus established a new courtliness of interior space. In these hushed, tingly atmospheres of withheld outburst, the visitor feels vaguely incriminated, while any object under the alarm's scan acquires an aura of baleful superlegitimacy. Consider, for example, an encounter with an institutional treasure like the Mona Lisa, one of the first artworks accoutered with alarms. You arrive through guarded corridors amid a restrained, pensive crowd. You take your turn and stand beneath the masterpiece, pondering deeply, awaiting its aesthetical effects. As you wait, you notice how old it looks, how remote and small. The longer you stare, the more its value seems manifest not in the dim little rectangle of crackulating paint, but in the assault-proof glass, the surveillance cameras, the softly militarized setting. Peering closer now, as if through freshly criminalized eyes, you imagine the alarm behind the portrait itself, the alarm surely underlying that famous, bemused face like a suppressed scream that twitches delicately at the corners of her mouth: One touch and she shrieks, one bump and her role in the history of art is instantly superseded by her role in the history of property and punishment.

Whether guarding a store window, then, or a priceless work of art, alarms illustrate the appeal to force implicit in the very concept of property. Yet if the interior security system advanced this coercive function to new heights, the alarms themselves remained as stationary and wire-fixtured as the earliest bur-glar-buzzers. It was only with the development of the transistor in the late fifties and the advent of smaller, wireless parts that alarms assumed a policing power as dispersed and flexible as property itself in a commodity-flooded world. With electronic components and plastic housings, no longer were alarms bound to place. Even the sounds, the twitters and whines, of this new "remote control" technology suggested a boundless penetration of external authority into internal conscience. By the end of the decade these qualities had been brought to ingenious perfection in the anti-shoplifting systems of the Sensormatic and Knogo corporations, whereby even the meagerest store merchandise could be tagged electronically with its own powers of adjudication and self-avenging squeals.

First installed in department stores in the sixties, such systems have become so common now that it is difficult for us to truly appreciate the horror they must have inspired in their first unwitting victims—that special, revelatory horror reserved for lab animals, infantry, and other prey of new machines.

Imagine yourself as an innocent young shopper in that dawn of the electronic age deliberating over some extravagant vendible—say, a costly pair of gloves. On an impulse you slip the gloves under your coat, cough, and glance around: so far, so good. Now with casual aplomb and excruciating restraint you saunter down the aisle, past the distracted clerks toward the store exit, your heart tugging and panting on its leash, trembling in the anticipation of life's most incomparable triumph: successful theft. The exit is just four, three, two steps away . . . . Then suddenly, a scream! A high-pitched, oscillating whine, as if some dentalish instrument were extracting the pulp of your very conscience. A guard steps forward and seizes you by the arm. And whatever your immediate fate, you will surely experience for years to come the after-twitches of this utter betrayal by the inanimate universe: like the fairy tale in which the broom or bucket—or in this case, the pricey gloves—suddenly springs to life, crying Thief! Thief! Thief!

As such high-tech ambushes proliferated through the sixties, they seemed at first to herald the

push-button totalitarianism grimly prognosticated in those days. Yet just as the path of human logic is so often unpredictable, so the technologies it dreams into existence rarely progress along clear trajectories. While hidden alarm networks continue to enclose more and more of our public space, the idea of a totally ordered, big-brotherly society now stands in our growing collection of antique futurisms. Where we once feared the perfection of social order, we now sense order fragmenting all around us. Suitably enough, then, the most recent phase of alarm development has a clearly discordant, regressive ring to it, as the sporadic howls of car alarms fill our city nights with echoes of the device's distant zoological origins.

Technically speaking, this latest "postmodern" genre of security alarm cannot be considered much of an advance. Yet more forcefully than any of its predecessors, the car alarm intones a central irony in the history of alarm technology. The automobile itself, as we know, represented the mechanical triumph of individual over collective. Enthroned in his roaming, honking intransigence, the motorist becomes a creature against all others. With alarms, this territorial self-acclaim can be sustained even when the motorist has called it a day. The early horn-triggering alarms of the seventies clearly evinced this surrogate function, emitting an autistically methodical honk like an enraged driver pounding his forehead on the horn. As later car alarms grew more ubiquitous and expressive, filling neighborhoods with their now-familiar idiom of whoooops, dweeeeps, and whirligig wails, they clearly demonstrated a paradox evident in so many areas of human progress: that our achievements tend to expand to the point of their own self-diminishment. Here the very line of technology first designed to protect the sanctity of the home has evolved into that sanctum's most persistent disrupter.

The history of security alarms, then, chronicles yet another case of social failures amplified by mechanical successes. On the purely technical side, the successes will undoubtedly proceed. In the line of detached alarms we already have accessory shriekers for luggage, pets, children, home-incarcerated felons, and habitually wandering victims of senility. In the field of security networks, we can envision future advances linking breakthroughs in digital encoding, bioengineering, and satellite surveillance. Whatever our minds can imagine owning we will surely find noisier ways to secure. Yet it is here that the limitations arise. For we have come far and acquired much since our earliest, dog-guarded days. Indeed, the world is now so thoroughly and irreversibly *owned* that each new generation arrives into a state of increasingly aggravated mutual trespass. And in such a state the laws configuring social relations appear to us more and more like a shrill, misfiring system of coercion into which we are all unwillingly deputized. In the end, we grow inured. For who today actually responds to these mechanical invokers of civic duty? When a car alarm shrieks under our window at night, don't we all simply curse, pack the pillows over our ears, and burrow back to sleep?. . . sleeping until startled awake by yet another alarm: the peep, jingle, or buzz of our bedside alarm clock, that most intimate of all security devices, the alarm by which property itself secures our daily labor, guarding its ever-expanding claims against the trespass of our dreams.

---

18 ½ Minute Gap

If there wasn't this interference
I could make myself perfectly clear
and the one who wants such clarity
would certainly be happy
if statues could be happy
and maybe they can (laughter)
because each one of us has to
identify with a statue sometimes
(or else there'd be no couples)
and even the lowliest among us
(I say, as if with all the authority
of experience behind me)
have to be happy sometimes
and who's to say it isn't
the statue part of us which feels such joy?
Well, me, but I too am another statue
(of a pigeon that shits on a statue)
and am only part of you if the sky is,
and it is, it is, and speculation
is this interference. But it's also Saturday.
Listen, children, all is not lost
and clear interference reminds me
that one can be drunk on soberness
and yesterday's desperate desire
to be simple again is, no doubt,
around here somewhere,
even if I am a crook.

—Chris Stroffolino

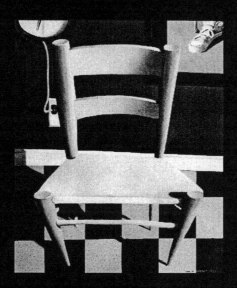

I Dreamed I Saw Joe Hill

STEPHEN DUNCOMBE

I dreamed I saw Joe Hill last night,
Alive as you and me.
Says I, "But Joe, you're ten years dead."
"I never died," says he.
"I never died," says he.

THERE was a time when major corporations didn't encourage us to "break the rules," business consultants didn't promote revolutions, and prominent neo-con historians didn't celebrate radical labor leaders. But the times, they are a-changin'. To wit:

Joe Hill was an organizer and songsmith for the anarcho-syndicalist Industrial Workers of the World in the first decades of this century. The Wobblies, as IWW members were called, were unrepentant revolutionaries, calling for "one big union" and the violent overthrow of capitalism. Arrested and convicted on trumped-up charges, Hill was executed by a firing squad in 1915.

Diane Ravitch is a historian who has built a successful career as an intellectual shill for the forces of public order that gunned Hill down. She served as assistant secretary of education in the Bush administration, has lectured around the world courtesy of our propaganda bureau, the United States Information Agency, and is currently a well-paid pen-pusher for the Brookings Institution and the Manhattan Institute, both influential establishment think tanks.

In the old days, never the twain would meet—except perhaps in battle. But open up Ravitch's popular 1990 *American Reader*, a compilation of "Words That Moved a Nation," and there's a song of Hill's, as well as Alfred Hayes's famous dream eulogy to the Wobbly. Hill is in good company in Ravitch's history textbook. Contrary to knee-jerk lefty expectations, this conservative doesn't ignore those whose politics differ from her own—she praises them. Her book of documents commemorates (in addition to the usual presidents and statesmen) some of the greatest radicals in American history: freelance revolutionary Tom Paine, Native American Chief Seattle, abolitionists Frederick Douglass and Henry Highland Garnet, feminists Sojourner Truth and Elizabeth Cady Stanton, socialist Eugene Debs, and Hill's comrade-in-verse, Woody Guthrie. In the pages of what Ravitch says she hopes will be a *McGuffey's Reader* for our time lie W. E. B. Du Bois and Langston Hughes; Tom Hayden and environmentalist Rachel Carson; Martin Luther King Jr., Jesse Jackson and Harvey Milk. Although Ravitch is a card-carrying member of the establishment, her American history reader is virtually an honor roll of American dissidence.

When we think of official history, of course, we usually think of books that honor a different type of greatness: the destiny of the country and the men who ruled it. Books where the winners are hailed with reverence while the losers are dismissed to the margins or pushed off the page entirely. "[I]t is but little more than two centuries since the oldest of our states received its first permanent colony," is the line with which George Bancroft introduced his 1834 *History of the United States*, perhaps the classic text of the genre. "Before that time the whole territory was an unproductive waste . . . . Its only inhabitants were a few scattered tribes of feeble barbarians, destitute of commerce and of political connection."

Historians like Bancroft had little time for "barbarians" like Chief Seattle; they were busy exalting those who won the games of "commerce and political connection." *Historical Tales and Golden Deeds*, a history primer from *The Boys and Girls Bookshelf* of 1912, made this emphasis clear from the start:

WHAT IS HISTORY?

Now, look carefully at the word HISTORY. From the letters in it you can make several words, but only two of them are of interest to us just now. The first three letters HIS, and the last five letters make the word STORY. Isn't it strange that history is largely made up of HIS STORY?

Strange indeed. While the authors of *Historical Tales and Golden Deeds* clear up this mystery by assuring us that history is *his story* because "history is made up mostly of the DEEDS OF GREAT MEN," others were not so easily convinced.

In the early sixties a new generation of historians turned in a different direction for answers. History, they argued, was not merely composed of golden deeds of great men, but arose from the clash of conflicting interests and collective struggle. No longer content to record the exploits of the privileged and the powerful, these new historians focused instead on the words and experiences of those often forgotten: workers, blacks, women, radicals. Turning the old focus upside-down, they aimed to write "history from the bottom up."

The reasons for the historians' break with tradition were many: the arrival of working-class, non-WASP, and female students into the academy who wanted to write their stories; expanded subject matter capable of occupying the record numbers of history Ph.Ds being churned out; and, of course, the fact that the new historians were right—history *is* often the story of dissidents and everyday people. But it was politics that provided the primary motivation for this new history. The fathers of this movement—E.P. Thompson, Eric Hobsbawm, Herbert Gutman—were themselves deeply involved in radical politics. By writing history from the bottom up they hoped to give the losers—that is, most of us—back our heritage.

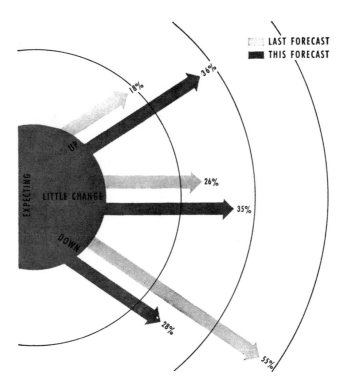

LAST FORECAST
THIS FORECAST

EXPECTING

UP
LITTLE CHANGE
DOWN

18%
36%
26%
35%
28%
55%

We could learn political lessons from the past, it was believed, and salvage successful models of struggle for the future.

Still, the best-selling history book of the sixties was Admiral Samuel Eliot Morison's *Oxford History of the American People,* in which "the people" were still defined by the deeds of great men, and in which arch cold warrior John Foster Dulles was mentioned eight times while W. E. B. Du Bois never came up at all. But over the next three decades the trends in American historiography shifted. Today, only hacks write about the great men. Historical studies of industry and of corporate practice have largely disappeared, while the shelves of hip bookstores overflow with inspiring tales of the little people and their hardships. It looks like our side won.

But the conversion of an establishment-funded historian like Ravitch to the cause of "people's history" should indicate to us that all is not as it seems in historiography-land. As should the fact that her publisher is HarperCollins—a property of Rupert Murdoch's News Corporation—make it clear that something else has shifted in the past thirty years.

Thompson, Hobsbawm, and Gutman—and, for that matter, Ravitch—were moved by politics; HarperCollins is guided by demographics, the market logic that dictates that you cannot sell a mass-culture product that categorically

This is "Commie Unionism"

excludes the majority of the population. The market segment of wealthy white men is just too small. If you want to sell to a mass market you had better represent the masses. This logic has spawned a vast body of corporate multiculturalism, including such curiosities as Mobil Oil's recent campaign urging customers to "Fill Up On Black History" at their service stations. And in *The American Reader* you get America the Rainbow, representing the diversity of the country and its consumer base.

"As we get to know the history of our society and hear the voices of those who created our energetic, complicated, pluralistic, and humane culture," Ravitch writes sensibly in her introduction, "we will understand ourselves and our times better." But Ravitch's goals are better understood not so much by her book's vast inclusiveness but by the surprising group that she neglects to include: the people on top. Nowhere in Ravitch's book will you find mention of the American Le-

gion, which lynched Joe Hill's colleagues, the Ku Klux Klan, which terrorized African Americans, or the National Association of Manufacturers, which coordinated countrywide campaigns against unionization. Powerful and influential worthies like Dulles, A. Mitchell Palmer, and J. Edgar Hoover, great persecutors of revolutionaries all, simply don't exist. Nor, needless to say, is there a whisper from modern-day captains of the culture trust like Murdoch. While the underdogs are everywhere triumphant, the overlords have disappeared.

Nowhere is this omission from *The American Reader* more glaring than in Ravitch's presentation of *Plessy v. Ferguson*, the infamous 1896 Supreme Court decision regarding the right of the state of Louisiana to segregate rail passengers by race. As it happens, the Supreme Court voted seven-to-one to uphold the Louisiana law, endorsing the myth of "separate but equal," and ushering in the era of

Jim Crow in the South. But what does *The American Reader* include? The lone dissent of Justice John Marshall Harlan, and not a word from the decision that was to stand for the next sixty years.

This tendency to ignore the forces that our new heroes fought against is not something Ravitch invented. On the contrary, it's a failing repeated throughout the social-history genre. But while the leftist scholars who invented the new history turned their attention to the powerless because they assumed the powerful would always have their hagiographers, one senses that Ravitch just saw a golden cultural-strategic opportunity: By making a tiny concession to trendy methodology she could score an enormous ideological victory. The people get to be noisily affirmed, sure, but power gets something much, much better: invisibility.

Like histories from the past, Ravitch's reader is a story of progress and destiny. Abolition, unionization, women's rights: A struggle is fought, great words are said, and then on to the next cause. History is a parade of good people fighting the good fight, a string of victories that made this country the great nation it is today. A more accurate assessment, of course, would be that the distinctly ungreat state of our nation today has more to do with their defeat than their victory. The one big union that Joe Hill died for hasn't come to pass; we're heading toward one big corporation instead.

But the corporation, and its leaders and lackeys, have receded into the shadows, pulling strings yet never appearing from behind the curtain. Certainly the National Association of Manufacturers and J. Edgar Hoover "moved a nation" more than a Wobbly song writer, but reading Ravitch's book you'd never know it. The powers-that-be don't exist. There is no elite in America. We are all Joe Hill.

For the historians who first pushed for history from the bottom up, the conflict between the powerless and the powerful was front and center. It was the context in which dissenting words and actions made sense. But as with almost everything else in our freewheeling, image-swapping, postmodern wonderland, this material context of struggle has evaporated. Rebellion has been neatly isolated from rebellion-against-what. Now Martin Luther King can give a speech on a Microsoft commercial, while Newt Gingrich fondly quotes social reformers. A lineage is magically extended from Joe Hill's war against capitalism to the noble corporation's struggle against "big labor." Beleaguered politicians are up against powerful welfare mothers and neocon pundits fight the good fight against tenured radicals.

"In a democratic society," Ravitch writes, explaining the logic behind her selections, "the power of persuasion is a necessary ingredient of social change." True enough, but in a society where the jackboot is frowned upon, the "power of persuasion" is just as necessary an ingredient of social order.

"The crowd is in the saddle," public relations pioneer Ivy Lee declared in 1916, warning a gathering of railroad executives of the irresistibly rising tide of democracy. Finding ways to control the great American mob has since become the none-too-subtle object of much of our mass culture, flattering our forgotten leaders, hailing our noble dreams, encouraging our efforts for self-improvement, and keeping the machinery of power carefully out of our sight and our reach. The victors still get to write the history books, but in the age of consumer democracy they no longer write about themselves—they write about us.

It's time to write about them, to write about presidents and statesmen, business associations and think tanks, CEOs and neo-con intellectuals. To revive that old-fashioned history from the top down— but from the perspective of the people on the bottom. The day before he was executed, Joe Hill wired Big Bill Haywood, the head of the IWW, with the message, "Don't waste any time in mourning. Organize." Hill has been dead for more than eighty years. Let him lie. We need to concentrate on the system that killed him.

Dreams Incorporated

Living the Delayed Life with Amway

MATT ROTH

W*HAT IS YOUR DREAM?* demanded a booming voice. The ballroom went dark and the audience settled in for a 15-minute video catalogue of the stuff dreams are made of: a blur of luxury cars, sprawling mansions, frolicking children, pristine beaches, hot-dogging jet-skiers, private helipads, and zooming jets—all set to caffeinated, John-Teshy instrumental music. The voice returned: "It's about *family!*" (A shot of kids collapsing on an oceanic lawn, love-tackled by Dad.) "It's about *security!*" (A shot of a palatial house.) "It's about *you!*" (A close-up of toes, gently lapped by the incoming tide, wriggling in white sand.)

This was Dream Night, and it was about Amway.

There are some one and a quarter million Amway members in the United States, roughly one for every two hundred of the rest of us, all of them eager to spread the gospel of salvation-through-selling-Amway-products. Considering Amwayers' penchant for compiling long lists of names, accosting strangers, and generally striving to collapse the degrees of separation

between them and other humans, the chances of an American being asked to an Amway meeting are quite good—somewhere between having a condom break during sex and being dealt a straight in a hand of poker. For a certain segment of the struggling middle class, where there's a magic mixture of disposable income and status insecurity, the odds are nearer those of catching a cold. And for someone like me, a post-collegiate pre-professional with a solid future in temping, Amway is more or less a mandatory rite of passage.

Dream Night was not the first Amway event I had been to, but it was the most hallucinatory. It began with the triumphal entrance of the Amway Diamond couples, half-jogging through a gauntlet of high-fives to the theme from *Rocky*, as the audience whooped and hollered and twirled their napkins over their heads. When the standing ovation finally tapered off, the emcee offered a prayer thanking God for (a) the fact that we lived in a free enterprise system, where there were no government agents kicking down the doors of meetings like Dream Night and (b) His Blessed Son. As dinner wound down, the video screens displayed a picture of what the guy next to me was quick to identify as a $20,000 Rolex watch. (He went on to tell of a fellow he knew who had a *$30,000* Rolex and who couldn't tell the time for the glare of the gold and diamonds.)

As its hands reached "midnight," the Rolex dissolved into a series of video montages depicting the consumer Shangri-La that our own forthcoming Amway success would open for us. We leered as a day in the life of a typical jobholder—all alarm clocks, traffic jams, and dingy cubicles—was contrasted with that of an Amway distributor, who slept in and lounged the day away with his family. We gawked hungrily as real-life Amway millionaires strutted about sprawling estates (proudly referred to as "family compounds") and explained that such opulence was ours for the asking. We chortled as a highway patrolman stopped an expensive sports car for speeding— only to ride away a moment later with an Amway sample kit strapped to his motorcycle. Our laughter became a roar of delight as the camera zoomed in on the sports car's bumper sticker: "JOBLESS . . . AND RICH!"

Interspersed with Dream Night's audiovisual assaults were six Castro-length harangues, which toggled along in a sort of good coach, bad coach routine: One youngish Amway Diamond would assure us that *we could do it!*, after which an older, sterner Diamond hectored us to stop making excuses for *not* doing it. The evening closed as we all

held hands and sang "God Bless America"—and then broke into a triumphal cheer.

The Amwayers who had brought me to Dream Night were flying high on the drive home, whooping occasionally just to vent their exhilaration. I felt as though I had just sat through a year's worth of infomercials, with some high school pep rallies and a few Tony Robbins lectures thrown in. But to see all this as an exercise in mass hypnosis, according to Amway's literature, would be to "misunderstand" what is, simply, "the best business opportunity in the world"—an assessment, strangely enough, with which the rest of world is starting to agree.

The Best Business Opportunity in the World

THE Amway Corporation was founded in 1959, ostensibly as a small-scale manufacturer of "biodegradable" detergents (beginning with Liquid Organic Cleaner, the patent for which Amway acquired from a struggling Detroit scientist). It has since grown into a $6 billion-a-year consumer-products behemoth selling everything from groceries to lingerie to water filtration systems. These products aren't available in stores, though. The key to Amway's success is its curious distribution system: Instead of using retail outlets and mass-media advertising, Amway licenses individual "distributors" to sell its goods from their homes. The distributors are independent franchisees; they buy products from Amway at wholesale and resell them at the "suggested retail" price, pocketing the difference as profit. Distributors are also paid a percentage of their sales (from 3 percent to 25 percent) by Amway itself. But the detail that distinguishes Amway's "multilevel marketing" scheme is that it rewards distributors for bringing new recruits into the sales force. Distributors get a cut not only of their own sales revenues, but of sales made by their recruits, their recruits' recruits and their recruits' recruits' recruits, a branching pyramid of lineally descended Amwayers known as a distributor's "downline."

The Amway approach supposedly avoids impersonal door-to-door sales, as each distributor need only sell directly to a small customer base of friends and family. Business "growth"—and an ascent to the flashier "bonus levels" (Ruby, Emerald, Diamond, Executive Diamond, Double Diamond, Crown Ambassador)—comes mostly through expanding one's downline. In theory, this odd marketing system ensures that benefits accrue not to Madison Avenue slicksters, but to ordinary folk capitalizing on their close-knit community ties—a scheme that seemingly reflects the small-town, Protestant populism of Amway's co-founders, Rich DeVos and Jay VanAndel.

Such pandering to heartland values has (along with record-breaking donations from Rich DeVos) endeared Amway to the Republican Party. But the company has also had its share of critics. In the seventies a succession of defectors charged that The Business (as the faithful call it) was a pyramid scheme, a fraudulent enterprise that made money by recruiting new members and channeling their fees to higher-ups in the organization. A 1979 Federal Trade Commission investigation concluded that Amway was not in fact a pyramid scheme—only that some of its claims to prospective distributors were overly optimistic—because most of its revenue came from sales of actual products.[1] But that didn't end the company's troubles. During the Reagan years, Amway was the butt of jokes and the target of exposés. Senior distributors set up private "distributor groups," organizations dealing in motivational materials and notorious mass rallies.[2] Dexter Yager, founder of the Yager Group, was known to leap around stages brandishing a giant gold crucifix.

Amway blamed its seamy image on a few "bad apples," impossible to avoid in a business that is open to all. (When Procter & Gamble, a competitor in the soap business, sued Amway for spreading rumors that P&G was a hotbed of Satanism, Amway shifted the blame to overenthusiastic distributors.) Since the eighties, the corporation has dealt with the issue by encouraging distributor groups to train Amwayers in "professionality," and by promulgating elaborate rules of conduct and a code of ethics for distributors.

The reform efforts seem to have paid off. Today Amway is portrayed as a model business.

A spate of articles in newspapers around the country have crowned "multilevel distribution" the Third Wave of marketing: If it looks like Amway, we're now told, then it's *not* a scam. Trade magazines laud Amway as a high-quality manufacturer; the United Nations has given it a rare Environmental Award; Jay VanAndel, the recipient of a score of business awards, served a term as president of the U.S. Chamber of Commerce; Ted Koppel has cited Rich DeVos as one of America's premier philanthropists; Larry King blurbed DeVos' book, *Compassionate Capitalism*, as "a credo for all people everywhere." Even the *Wall Street Journal*, which delights in mild ridicule of Amway spectacles, never completely laughs off The Business. The paper is always careful to mention Amway's billions in annual sales, the new class of professionals flocking to it, the FTC decision ruling it legal, and its remarkable global expansion—especially in Eastern Europe.

But Dream Night brought all the questions back to the surface: If Amway isn't a scam, why did it seem so much like one? It may win heaps of praise nowadays, but Amway doesn't seem to have changed much at all. Perhaps what's changed is us. While Amway is the same as it ever was, the rest of us have made peace with commercial insanity. Maybe capitalism has finally reached the stage of self-parody, unblushingly cel-

ebrating a house-of-cards as its highest achievement. And maybe Dream Night, instead of being the ritual of a fringe cult, is the vanguard of the future.

First Look

FITTINGLY, my encounter with Amway began during a long-term temp assignment at Andersen Consulting's ENTERPRISE 2020 project, an ongoing exhibit to which consultants would bring potential clients to scare them about the future. The main attraction was a battery of "industry experts" who produced customized nightmare scenarios to help manufacturing executives from across the globe see the Third Wave coming at them. The experts would discourse gravely about globalization, accelerating technology, managed chaos, self-organizing supply chains, flex-this, flex-that, and nano-everything, eventually arriving at the message of this elaborate sideshow: The future is not to be faced without an Andersen consultant on retainer.

Sales pitch though it was, E2020 subscribed to a worldview that's now ubiquitous in the wider culture. Its central metaphor was overheatedly Darwinian—the global economy as nature run riot, lush for the dominant, unforgiving for the slow to adapt—but also strikingly theological. In the next millennium, a resurgent Market would act as the vengeful (invisible) hand of God, laying waste to the Second Wave's many Towers of Babel—government planning, welfare states, unions, warehouses, consolidated factories, even mega-conglomerates. Thus, "progress" required that we bury our arrogant bids for security and clear the ground for a new order of pure Nietzschean struggle.

I don't know how the CEOs stumbling through E2020 felt about this, but from what I could gather, the prospects for people like me were distinctly mixed. On the one hand, as a customer I'd be awesomely empowered—whole industries would rise and fall according to the butterfly effect generated by tiny shifts in consumer taste. But as a worker I'd be downgraded to "enabled." I would have to eschew "third party" union representation, sacrifice guaranteed benefits, dispense with government protections, and forgo lifelong employment; instead, I'd accumulate "human capital" to sell in an open labor market. Of course, "change" would repeatedly render that arduously amassed human capital obsolete in the space of a nanosecond, after which I was to uncomplainingly set about accumulating more. This was called "being adaptable."

The forecast looked pretty grim, and I wasn't the only one who thought so. My supervisor, Sherri, also seemed to have succumbed to E2020's mood of millennial angst. As events coordinator for E2020, responsible for making each client's time in Chicago—from the catered lunch to the after-hours excursion— "exceed their expectations," Sherri's job was already very twenty-first century in its focus on pampering those with means. She was perfect for the role, a seamless blend of prim professional and girlish emo-

tion-worker. Tall, blond, and angular, she had deep-set Nordic eyes that gave her an air of maturity—unless she was excited, when they would widen improbably, revealing the spirit of a child lost in wonder. One minute she was commanding a team of caterers, the next she was dissolving into giggles, waving her arms and squealing with excitement. On top of her sixty-plus hours a week at E2020, she was improving herself with MBA classes at night; she, too, was seeking some way off the wobbly treadmill of income-from-wages-salaries-and-tips. When Amway called, touting a future that combined business ownership with 100 Percent Empowered Consumerism, she was ready.

One day, Sherri asked me to attend a meeting at which a "millionaire from the West Coast" was to talk about "business trends of the nineties." I was not entirely caught by surprise— Sherri had dropped hints about starting her own "distribution business" at about the time that Amway Dish Drops appeared in the E2020 kitchen—and although she didn't tell me the millionaire was from Amway, it wasn't difficult to guess which version of the gospel of wealth he'd be preaching. I jumped at the chance to meet this mysterious man of money, although from totally insincere motives— the old anthro major in me was hankering for a bona fide subculture to gawk at.

The meeting was hosted by Sherri's friend Josh and his wife Jean[3], he a commodities broker, she a high school math teacher. Sherri and Josh had attended the same small Christian college. Before that, he had been an Indiana farm boy, and he still had the look: a beefy, boyish face with a grin that verged on gaping, mussed hair with perpetually sweaty bangs, a brown suit that flared in all the wrong places, and a general air of guilelessness. This cast in high relief his constant, ill-advised attempts to put on city airs: the firm handshake, the breezy small talk, the man-of-the-world asides.

Scott Coon (the millionaire from Seattle), on the other hand, was the genuine article: *His* breezy small talk projected an illusion of sincere interest, his well-fed face reflected self-assurance. Scott worked the small crowd with consummate slickness. After a mumbled intro from Josh (followed by whoops from the audience), Scott stood beaming at us, rubbing his hands in anticipation.

This was a "First Look"—the initial meeting where Amwayers bring prospects to scare them about the future—and Scott delivered it with gusto and verve. Sherri had told me to expect an hour-long talk, but two and a half hours barely winded this speaker. He delivered 150 minutes of fast patter without notes, and touched upon such diverse topics as the high divorce rate, the quality of McDonald's hamburgers, IBM's strategy of diversification, and the number of cupholders in the minivan he had recently bought *with cash*. I would later realize that this was a typical Amway speech: somewhere between an infomercial and a sermon, a loosely organized string of riffs that bespoke either improvisational genius or, more likely, countless repetitions.

Scott spent the first hour explaining America's economic crisis, which is rooted in a betrayal stretching back to the late nineteenth century. See, that's when big corporations, with the help of government-run public education, first convinced Americans to abandon their entrepreneurial instincts and accept jobs. Before that, everyone was either a small-business owner or apprenticing to be one; afterwards, it was all about benefits packages. Emasculated by wage slavery, Americans had muddled along fairly well until, as stagflation rent the land in the 1970s, we realized in horror that mere wages were helpless against "exponentially expanding" costs.

Scott confidently reprised decades' worth of conservative alarmism, invoking inflation and national debt and other flat-earth bugbears in a doomsday routine as charmingly archaic as it was fatuous. An accurate narrative of the last few decades—growing productivity, GDP, and per-capita income, accompanied by a massive upward redistribution of wealth—would hardly have packed the millennial portent Scott was looking for. The Second Wave, like Communism, like all the works of man, was destined to decay and collapse, making way for the coming entrepreneurial kingdom—which, for those who lacked faith or zeal, would bring a day of reckoning. Were we *ready*? To prove he "wasn't making this crazy stuff up," he littered the floor with copies of *Fortune, Money,* and *Forbes*, citing the relevant disaster stories. I felt like I was back at ENTERPRISE 2020.

But unlike E2020, which catered to the executive class, Scott offered salvation to the common worker, the middle-level manager, the petit bourgeois professional. Moreover, he offered them something so entrepreneurial, so Third Wave, so purely capitalist that it transcended Darwinian struggle, allowing people to escape into early retire-

ment. He held up a copy of *Success* magazine trumpeting the "Young and Rich in America." "It's still possible to make it in this country," he declared. "There's no hammer and sickle over this deal yet!"

He was about to show us the sure bet in the coming high-stakes society.

The Plan

BEFORE the meeting, I had worried that my hand-held tape recorder would stand out. As it happened, everyone was recording Scott: I kept track of time by the sounds of cassettes being flipped. I was on Side B of a 90-minute tape before Scott dropped the word "Amway," and I was on another cassette entirely before I captured the heart of the "best business oppor-

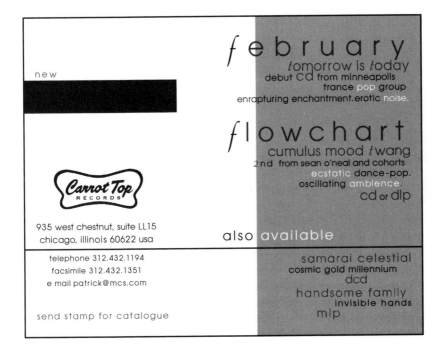

tunity in the world": the Amway Sales & Marketing Plan. This was not, however, a topic to be discussed without considerable preparatory spadework.

The Sales & Marketing Plan is based on what Scott called "the revolutionary business strategy of *duplication*." To illustrate the idea he pointed to an imperfect example: McDonald's, which succeeded so phenomenally, Scott explained, thanks to duplication—not because it served particularly good food (people who "hadn't spent a lot of time around millionaires" always amused Scott with their idea that successful businesses required quality products). Ray Kroc had figured out a better way to flip a burger, but instead of hiring employees to do it, he taught it to franchisees, people fired up with the zeal of business ownership. While they willingly slaved to make what they owned more valuable, Kroc made his money by "taking a penny for teaching others how to make a dollar." His was truly a magical income, expanding whether he worked for it or not, growing whether he lived or died. Long after Kroc had "taken a dirt bath," Scott joked, duplication still supported his widow to the tune of $200 million a year!

But the problem with "public franchises" like McDonald's, Scott noted, is that they only allow one person to enjoy this enchanted income. "Private" or "multilevel" franchises, on the other hand, allow people at all levels to dupli-

cate themselves. Everyone begins as a grit-teeth franchise operator, but by "sharing their business with others" they would come into an exponentially expanding avalanche of wealth large enough to outrun the ballooning costs of twentieth-century life.

Scott's own income, he assured us, was "out of control"—and, furthermore, it wasn't built on something as old-fashioned as food. He worked in the cutting-edge field of distribution, where the real money was to be made nowadays. Through his business, he could get thousands of quality goods, many of them brand names, and cut distribution costs by almost a third. The company that organized this system did $6 billion a year in sales (Scott helped us to understand this awesome figure by describing for us the height of a billion-dollar stack of hundred-dollar bills) and was, on top of this, debt-free. It might surprise us that this company was Amway![4]

As its Sales & Marketing Plan demonstrated, there were two ways to make money in Amway. You could buy products cheap (at wholesale costs reportedly 30 percent below retail) and sell them dear; or, more lucratively, you could share The Business with others, and build your own empire of "downlines." Since Amway awards bonuses to its distributors based on their wholesale volume, and since each distributor's wholesale figures includes the sales made by his or her "downlines," each convert to the Amway cause would enlarge his or her own incomes. To see how this worked, we were told to imagine recruiting six distributors, each of whom would bring in four more, who in turn would each net an additional two. Our downlines, according to this "6-4-2" formula, would then have 78 members. If each of our underlings did $100 a month in sales, we'd be making an extra $2,000 a month in bonuses.[5]

And for those of us who had no taste for sales, Scott had fabulous news: A group of Amway millionaires had come up with a sure-fire system for making The Plan work—and had formed World Wide Dreambuilders LLC, a corporation independent of Amway, to teach that system to others. All that was required to ensure an Amwayer's success, Dreambuilders taught, was that each distributor simply bought $100 of Amway products a month for his own "personal use." That meant no high-pressure pitches, no Tupperware parties—no sales at all, in fact. You could meet your $100 monthly goal by selling to *yourself*—at 30 percent off retail to boot! Being an intensive Amway consumer was such a great deal that once we spread the word, our businesses would practically build themselves. We could quickly 6-4-2 to that extra $2,000, and once our six "legs" did likewise, we'd be pulling in $50,000 a month; if we included some other "factors," more like $100,000! And that was just the beginning: There were some truly spectacular incomes to be made through The Business—which Scott would have told us about but for FTC regulations barring him from doing so.

In Dreambuilders' version of The Plan one could glimpse an es-cape from the coming economic dead-end through empowered consumption. We'd have all the twenty-first-century cred of working (and shopping) from home, engaging in cutting-edge marketing, being part of a decentralized network, and nurturing our inner entrepreneur. And all the human capital we needed was the ability to shop and be effusive about it, which were practically American birthrights.

But judging by the Herculean efforts made to seduce me into The Business, the Plan couldn't be quite as effortless as it sounded. Josh and Jean, who had now thrown themselves into signing me up as one of their "downlines," had adopted a strategy that consisted mainly of driving me, at untold inconvenience to themselves, to as many meetings as possible (they were all in far-flung suburbs, so I needed the rides). My attempts to find refuge in the back of the car being firmly rebuffed by Jean, I sat captive in the passenger seat while Josh tried out the various small-talk friendship-building techniques he'd learned from World Wide. Our trips always ended with Josh proffering a Sample Kit, a large white box filled with detergents and propaganda, including *Promises to Keep*, a book by the suggestively named Charles Paul Conn, as well as xeroxed articles explaining why Amway was the most "misunderstood

company in the world." I resisted Josh's offers; I was reluctant to take the Amway plunge and knew that the real purpose of the kit was to give him an excuse to drop by my house and retrieve it.

I also had doubts about the business of The Business. Amway products didn't seem to be winging off the shelves. Sherri complained that she couldn't even get her own family to buy from her business: Her mother preferred to go to the local Costco. ("A *communist* store! Gee *thanks*, Mom!") Relying on intimates wouldn't be enough, she explained; the real way to build The Business was to "make casual acquaintances out of strangers." The techniques for doing this, which often resembled pick-up lines, were an important part of Dreambuilders' curriculum. Josh spoke of his admiration for Diamond Distributor Randy Sears, who had come up with all sorts of "ice-breakers": He'd pretend to know someone, for instance, and they'd often pretend to know him right back. Or he'd walk right up to somebody and say, "I like your belt!"[6]

In their zeal, Josh and Jean shuttled me to at least one meeting too many. The worst was a Seminar, an afternoon of "professional training" definitely geared to insiders. Here, during a marathon transfusion of spine-stiffening resolve, I got a glimpse of just how demoralizing the travails of Amway could be. The speaker, Conrad Halls, a Hollywood cameraman

with over-the-hill golden-boy looks, had been frank and congenial in his First Look the night before. His debunking of negative Amway stereotypes included the almost touching refrain, "I hope you don't think I flew 3,000 miles to show you *that* kind of business," spoken with a candid stare and open, outstretched arms.

Conrad was much sterner in the Seminar's light of day. He emphasized that Amway was not a get-rich-quick scheme, that the "difference between *trying* and *triumphing* is a little *umph*," and that—and here he pointed to his head—if you didn't already have a positive attitude, you'd better "reprogram your computer" quick! He praised a woman in the audience who was missing her daughter's birthday party to attend the Seminar. She lived what Amwayers call a "delayed life." "In a few years, when you're spending all day, every day with your daughter, you'll look back at this investment into your business," he reassured the woman, "and know it was the best birthday gift of all." Those who slacked in their attendance of World Wide functions, he warned, might just as well forget about being successful. After this short homily, Conrad's wife Lisa pleaded with female Seminar-goers to be more professional in their handling of distribution (uh-oh), and added an important caveat to her husband's notion of the delayed life: If you're discouraged at the outset of your Amway career, if you somehow doubt the whole thing, don't let it show. Instead, "fake it till you make it."

It was not an adage that inspired confidence. The Seminar's desperate atmosphere, its feel of too much good money thrown after bad, reinforced my doubts. I began to sense that Amway did not grow organically, as a result of the great bargains it offered wholesale buyers on its fine products, but rather by a process of recursive "faking it": screwed people trying to get unscrewed by screwing others. I couldn't know for sure, of course, until I saw the wholesale price list and could judge for myself just how much money I could save by buying through Amway. But the price list, ostensibly Amway's big selling point, was the one document that Josh always neglected to have in his briefcase.

One night, after he had taken me out to dinner (we went Dutch), Josh told me that there was a price list in the back of his car—sealed in an Amway Starter Kit. I could have it right away; I just had to give him the $160 fee to officially join Amway. Uncertain about taking the plunge, I claimed my checking account couldn't cover $160 that week. That was all right, he insisted: I could write a post-dated check that he would hold until I gave the O.K. to deposit it. I still resisted, and he got out of the car with me, opening the hatch to show me the sealed white box within. Eventually, he settled for giving me a book called *Being Happy,* which he could later retrieve.

The next week, I decided. I would never learn the truth about Amway until I joined. I left a message on Josh's Amvox voicemail telling him I had the $160 check ready. A week later, I left another message. By my third attempt, I got Josh himself (who had been intending to return my calls) and was finally able to arrange a time to separate me from my money. It wasn't the last time I felt he and Jean weren't exactly cut out for the rigors of The Business.

Buying Through The Business

AMWAYERS are like vampires: To join them, you must invite them into your home. Unpacking the Starter Kit was mainly Jean's show, she being the most balanced of my upline trio, the calmest and least prone to outbursts of enthusiasm. (Josh limited himself to preparing my contract and casting a longing gaze every time my roommate ventured out of his room.) Jean was also the only one who had actually read the Amway Business Manual (included in the Kit). Nonetheless, she deferred to Josh: He did the "more important" work of "building" The Business, while she performed the womanly tasks of customer service.

She showed me how all the dilution bottles worked (Amway liquid cleaners come in "superconcentrated" form, which makes them superinconvenient to use), and took me on a tour of eight or so catalogues, pointing out all the products I would want to make an effort to learn about. Finally, she did the best she could with the Amway paperwork, but, math teacher though she was, she got lost in its byzantine intricacies. "I'm still learning," she ex-

plained with an embarrassed smile. "But it's O.K., because once I get it all down, it's all I'll ever need to know, whether our business is a hundred dollars a month or a million!" Unfortunately, it was what I needed to know just to buy a roll of toilet paper.

Figuring out the arcana of Amway took months. The price list, for instance, is denominated in two artificial Amway currencies called "Point Value" (PV) and "Bonus Volume" (BV), which are listed alongside the U.S. dollar-denominated wholesale ("Distributor Cost") and "Suggested Retail" prices. But for all the arcana, the system's core concept was simple.

Imagine that you've struck a deal with a company to give you discounts for buying in bulk: If you buy $100 worth of stuff, they'll send you a 3 percent rebate. For $300 or more, it goes up to 6 percent, $600 or more, 9 percent, and so on up to $7,500 and 25 percent. Now, let's say you're unable to spend more than $100 a month, but manage to get 74 other people to go in with you. Together, you spend $7,500 and divide up the 25 percent rebate. Everyone saves money, and the rebate is shared equally. That's the idea behind a consumer co-op or wholesale buying club.

Now, let's say you get the 25 percent rebate from the company but tell the other 74 participants, "Look, you've each spent only $100, so you'll get only a 3 percent rebate." Not only would you save 25 percent on your purchases, but you make a 22 percent profit on everyone else's. *That's* the idea behind Amway.

In the canonical 6-4-2 pyramid, the "Direct Distributor" on top receives a 25 percent "Performance Bonus" on the entire group's spending.[7] The Performance Bonuses that go to his six "legs" (12 percent of their sub-groups' spending) are deducted from his own, leaving him with a 13 percent profit. In turn, they pay out 6 percent bonuses to their four "legs," who pay out 3 percent bonuses to their two. Those bottom 48 distributors, in other words, get back 3 percent of everything they spend while the top distributor gets 13 percent of everything they spend. (The amount of all checks are calculated, incidentally, by Amway's central computer and distributed by Amway; uplines don't actually write checks to their downlines.) It would amount to the same thing if the distributors at the bottom were to receive the 25 percent rebate—and then pay fees directly to their uplines equal to 3 percent, 6 percent, and 13 percent of their purchases.

Disguising the upward flow of fees within a downward flow of commissions definitely has its advantages. One of the decisive factors in the 1979 FTC decision exonerating Amway from allegations of pyramiding was that most of its revenues came from product sales, not from enrollment fees. The assumption is that those sales are based on rational consumer choices—made on the basis of price and quality—and that the money paid into the bonus system is not an extraneous surcharge, but merely the portion other corporations would pour into their marketing budgets. Amway claims, in fact, that it's able to save even its small-time distributors money by avoiding things like pricey mass advertising. These savings are the source of the alleged wholesale 30 percent Basic Discount that every distributor is supposed to enjoy even before the bonuses kick in.

To test these claims I took my new Amway wholesale price list down to the local supermarket for a price comparison. As it turned out, Amway *wholesale* prices were only slightly better than supermarket *retail* prices, although a few Amway products, like freezer bags, were significantly cheaper. And this was giving The Business the benefit of many doubts: I factored in its claim that its detergents are more "concentrated" than other brands; I compared Amway with high-quality brand-name products, not store brands or generics; and I compared only regular prices, ignoring the fact that the supermarket, unlike Amway, always has items on sale (not to mention coupons).[8] The same results obtained at the local drugstore in comparisons of vitamins and cosmetics. All in all, the 30 percent Basic Discount was nowhere to be found.[9]

To get the full Amway experience, I started buying my groceries through The Business. I found that, despite Amway's growth, its "cutting-edge" distribution system preserved all the pitfalls of a small buying club run out of somebody's

apartment. My local supermarket, ironically, actually did start as a buying club run out of someone's apartment in the 1930s; as it grew, however, it accreted all the efficiencies of the retail system. Now it's open 14 hours a day, seven days a week, with professional managers, stockers, and checkers; a visit there is quick and hassle-free. To make my "pick-up" at Josh and Jean's apartment, on the other hand, required an hour-long el ride and arrangements with a friend to haul the stuff back home, all scheduled only during those brief windows of opportunity when Josh and Jean could be there to meet me.

And these inconveniences pale beside the emotional shock of entering Josh and Jean's apartment. Not big to begin with, its thorough occupation by Amway Corporation made it positively claustrophobic. The living room was dominated by huge metal cabinets displaying Amway cleaning and food products; shelves along the wall were devoted to toiletries; boxes of cereal lined the top of the couch. Next to the window was an eraser board listing upcoming World Wide Dreambuilders meetings; free wall space and the outside of cabinets were decorated with motivational slogans ("I AM A WINNER!") drawn in crayon.

When I arrived for the first time, Jean had already bagged my order. She apologized for the absence of some items I had or-

dered, which were on "backorder." (Among them were the Big Fiber Fudgies, high-fiber brownies that Josh, Jean, and Sherri rated among the tastiest delectations on earth. Jean urged me to be brave about the Fudgie delay.)

Inefficiencies were everywhere, since the supply chain rigidly followed the line of recruitment. Some of the items I ordered had to be sent by mail all the way from Seattle, since that was where Scott and Shelley Coon, our upline Direct Distributors, happened to live. Others could be shipped from a regional warehouse in Michigan—one of Amway's attempts to make the system more workable—but still had to be ordered through the Coons. Some items—unavailable from the warehouse—could be sent directly to me via UPS, but my building didn't have a front desk to receive them. Jean suggested I have them sent to her apartment to be picked up with the rest of my order.

While Jean explained all of this, Josh, by way of chatting up the friend who was to drive me home, offered him some Glister Anti-Plaque Gum. This was a companion to Glister Anti-Plaque Toothpaste, something so caustic-sounding that I never dared put it in my mouth. "It's actually illegal in Canada," Josh improbably declared, adding, "I guess they just don't worry about plaque up there." Friend-with-Car excused himself to go to the bathroom, from which he

emerged with an odd look on his face. Once safely in the car he described the bathroom as something not to be missed.

I did pick-ups for several depressing weeks. Apart from Sherri, I never saw any sign of another customer. It was like one of those dusty, deathly-still mom-and-pops frequented only by regulars who come mainly to chat—and I was oppressed with a similar sense that the proprietors needed my money more than I needed their merchandise. It was actually a relief when, one week, Josh and Jean left town without warning me.

What with backorders and unexpected disappearances, it took me a few weeks to gather enough items for my next experiment: a blind taste-test pitting Amway food against brands from "communist" supermarkets. Unfortunately, biases crept into the data when my subjects learned to identify what they called the Telltale Amway Aftertaste, a lingering cardboard bouquet with unmistakable Pine-Sol inflections. Aftertaste aside, Amway food still rated low: Only the Critics' Choice Cherry Flavored Toaster Pastries (a Pop-Tart analog) managed to eke into second-to-last place. The Goglonian Bagels were universally declared the worst ever experienced. And the Big Fiber Fudgies? Let's just say that they were pretty much all Telltale Aftertaste.

Despite the mediocrity of Amway products, one can't help but be impressed by their sheer number and variety. Other multilevels offer one or two miracle products, such as nutritional supplements like blue-green algae or "minerals in colloidal suspension," etc., about which wild claims can be made with impunity. Such products defy conventional sales methods, usually because they require some sort of conversion experience on the part of the customer or elaborate person-to-person instruction. Amway, with its Liquid Organic Cleaner, began this way. But today Amway insists that *all* products are better sold through multileveling: couches, VCRs, cookies, socks, toilet paper, you name it. The Amway goal is not to push one wildly fraudulent product, but to offer a just barely convincing imitation of consuming life, allowing Amwayers to exhaustively shift all of their consumption to dues-paying mode.[10]

Dreambuilding

FROM time to time the absurdities and contradictions of The Business would surface in Josh's conversation. In one of his many unguarded moments, he voiced a preference for Amway Scrub Rite because it ran out more quickly than the "superconcentrated" Amway cleaners, enabling him to buy it more often. Catching himself, he quickly added, "Of course, it still lasts a *long time*." This puzzled me. Why was Josh so eager to shovel money at Amway? The rational thing would be to minimize his own purchases while strong-arming his downlines into buying as much as possible. But, of course, if everyone did that, the whole business would evaporate. This is Amway's central dilemma.

There were some rational explanations for Josh's behavior. To recruit others, he needed the propaganda talents of his upline World Widers, who made it clear that their underlings had to be "fanatical about personal use," and even held this up as an index of a distributor's positive attitude. Another rationale was provided by the well-worn anecdote, often retold in the first person, about the distributor who missed a new Performance Bracket by a few dollars when *a little bit more* personal use could have taken them over the edge. The story always ended, "Well, you better believe I never made *that* mistake again!"

But as I came to know Josh better, I realized he was acting not so much out of a calculated strategy as out of a deep faith in duplication. Josh believed that whatever he did, his downlines would imitate: If he set the example of filling his house with only "positive" (i.e. Amway) products, so would they. Rich DeVos, more philosophically, calls this the Law of Compensation: "In the long haul, every gift of time, money, or energy that you give will return to benefit you."

Josh felt that duplication worked in the other direction as well. If he emulated the multi-multi-millionaires ("multi-multi's" for short) above him—and did exactly what they said they had done—he would succeed as they had. In his mind, his interests were already merged with theirs. He would boast of *their* ac-

---

complishments, tell me how *their* bonuses just kept "getting better and better all the time!" For him, of course, bigger bonuses for uplines simply meant a more powerful drain on his income. But that kind of self-defeating "stinking thinking" missed the point, as far as Josh was concerned. By "visualizing" great wealth, by worshiping great wealth, and by imitating the consuming habits of the great and wealthy, he would somehow obtain great wealth.

I only learned the extent to which he and Jean had convinced themselves of this when I worked up the courage to visit their bathroom. It was a strange spectacle indeed. The wall opposite the toilet was decorated with Post-Its, each with a biblical proverb or chestnuts like "A drowning man doesn't complain about the size of the life preserver" and "If you don't stand for something, you'll fall for anything!" I was startled when a reggae song about "winners" suddenly filled the air; I located the speakers in the medicine cabinet. Most impressive, however, was a wish list taped above the toilet. Scrawled in pencil, it was presumably lengthened whenever Josh or Jean had a flash of covetousness in the shower. It included, among other items,

> A bathroom as big as our apartment and someone to clean it every other day (but not Sunday);
>
> A whirlpool as big as our bathroom;
>
> Seven pairs of tennis shoes and seven courts;
>
> A black helicopter seating 12;
>
> Horses, 21;
>
> A chateau, with seven gardens and seven fountains and a chauffeur.

Like my friend, I was struck by the fairy tale numerology that invested even tennis shoes with a mythic charge. In Amway, extravagant desire is *the* motive force: To desire what your upline has, even those things that nobody could realistically hope for, is what keeps the scheme in motion.[11] Josh and Jean's wish list, as well as the many other "visualization" exercises involved in dreambuilding, was simply part of their training to ever more expansively *want*. But to what end? What desire had propelled them into Amway in the first place?

Greed and power-lust, to be sure. But also something larger, more desperate. Americans have, after all, worked progressively longer hours since the Vietnam War; and job insecurity is a hallmark of our E2020 future. Amway promises to transcend the excesses of capitalism by wholeheartedly indulging them. At a time when realistic, collective solutions are off the docket, it's no surprise that people are turning to miracles. In this way, Amway is not so different from other mutations of the American Dream: the notion that grassroots entrepreneurs will save the urban poor, that the stock market will save Social Security, that casinos will fund our schools. All of

these schemes offer salvation while preserving a core myth of capitalism: that the instruments for distributing wealth are also responsible for creating it. Or as Double Diamond and Überparasite Greg Duncan put it at Dream Night in a talk about Washington bureaucrats dividing up the social pie, "I *make* pies!"

It's a myth that's hard to resist—insofar as the exchange floor and the casino offer dramatic visible spectacles of people getting rich while real wealth-creation is the arcane stuff of productivity figures and efficiency studies—but it has tragic consequences for people like Josh and Jean. Perfectly capable of leading enjoyable lives, they nonetheless surround themselves with Amway propaganda, subsist on Amway food, immerse themselves in Amway culture, think in Amway jargon, and siphon their income to Greg Duncan in the hopes of learning the "secret" of his wealth.

Saturation

As much as Josh ignored the contradictions of his faith, he could always be counted on to express them. A typical Joshism (uttered while describing the photos of new Directs that appear in the *Amagram* each month): "People are amazed that there are that many new Directs each month—at first, they think it's per year, but no!" The point apparently being the great odds of success.

Then, in the very next breath: "I look through them every month to make sure there aren't too many from Illinois. I'm worried that Chicago will get saturated. Last month, though, there were only two." Now he was selling the *poor* odds.

Amway is haunted by the specter of saturation, the success that spells disaster. The 6-4-2 scenario tells it all: To keep one promise of $2,000-a-month, seventy-eight more need to be made whose fulfillment is still pending. The problem is that growth doesn't improve this ratio: Were Amway to conquer the known universe, fewer than 2 percent of its distributors would be (or mathematically *could be*) Directs or higher. Of the rest, about 90 percent would be actively losing money—and without a pool of prospects to give them hopes for the future, they would surely quit. Amway would collapse from the bottom up.

The prospect is alarming enough that Charles Paul Conn, in *Promises to Keep*, works hard to prove it'll never happen. "The reality," he tells us, "is entirely different from what might be predicted by a statistician with a slide rule." He points to the millions of likely untapped prospects—youths, retirees, downsized professionals, foreigners—although he fails to acknowledge that recruiting them would only make the Business hungrier. More plausibly, he adds that Amway is a small part of the population and will stay that way. The Business's high dropout rate, he explains, though "often cited as a negative factor, actually serves to keep the pool of potential distributors large." In other words, Amway's salvation is its high rate of failure.

This hard truth belies Amway's populism, its promise that success depends merely on getting in on the ground floor, and that *every floor is the ground floor*. Deep down, Josh may have realized that an Amway easy enough for even him to master would soon self-destruct. This buried consciousness surfaced, for example, in the way he consoled himself with weird probability statistics. He knew how many levels deep he had to extend his downline (something like six) before he was certain to recruit someone with a knack for huckstering, providing a rising tide on which Josh could float. It was unlikely, of course, that a guy like Josh could spawn a six-level downline without the help of such a person, but that simply masked a deeper improbability: that there were enough of these theoretical master salesmen to go around to every schlub who couldn't succeed otherwise.

Ultimately, however, he dealt with his catch-22 through simple fantasies of escape. He was adamant that someday he'd be a millionaire, his current predicament no more than a bad memory. His hand would describe a hyperbola as he explained that The Business was hard at first, but if you'd just stick in there, you'd soon enjoy *exponential* success. This would happen so soon that he wouldn't have to prospect long enough even to get

particularly good at it. "The point is not to get good," he insisted, "It's to get done!"

Sadly, it was unlikely Josh would ever be one of the few to "get done." Amway doesn't thrive through exponential growth, but through the fanatical consumption of a relatively small number of people who believe that everyone can be a "winner."[12] Josh was in denial—and it was in Amway/World Wide's interest to keep him that way.

The Power of Association

AFTER a year in The Business, Josh and Jean were scarcely able to devote eight hours a week to distributing goods and showing The Plan—activities that required a good supply of prospects, customers, and downlines. They were desperate for new leads, also a scarce resource, and regularly alarmed me with proposals that we all go to some public place and *mingle*. Of course, that would have required overcoming shyness and other gag responses, impediments that Josh, Jean, and Sherri never really overcame (most of their leads seemed either to be family or, like me, co-workers.) They would, on the other hand, devote entire weekends to "recharging their batteries" at First and Second Looks, Seminars, Rallies, and Major Functions (Dream Night, Leadership Weekend, Family Reunion, Free Enterprise Day); meetings that required only in-

EVOLUTION ACCORDING TO AMWAY

security and neediness, which all three had in spades.

These functions, all of which were sponsored by World Wide Dreambuilders, were rhetoric-fests where Amway's self-help message was pushed to its logical addiction-recovery extreme—although with the roles curiously reversed. "J-O-B people," meaning those who were *not* Amway-style entrepreneurs, were portrayed as the helpless addicts, hooked on the "immediate gratification" of a weekly paycheck. It was *they* who were in denial, telling themselves that they didn't have a problem, that they were happy working all day for practically nothing. In contrast, the "delayed life" was a healthy process of withdrawal, of gradually replacing the "negatives" in your life (including non-Amway products) with "positives." Most importantly, you learned to "dream" again, reconnecting with the inner child who, before the 9-to-5 beat it down, had fantasized about big houses and fast cars.[13]

The 12-step shtick was a ready justification for the cult-like regimen of World Wide followers. Like alcoholics, wage junkies had to attend frequent meetings, supplemented with books and tapes, to keep on track; they had to dissociate themselves from bad influences, i.e. "broke" friends and relatives who would try to keep them down; they had to follow "Eight Core Steps" (four of which involved buying stuff from either Amway or World Wide Dreambuilders); and they

had to let go of their ego and overcome their fear of change, to open themselves to the counseling of their upline "sponsors." Sponsoring, as in Alcoholics Anonymous, was an act of love and healing. Your uplines would never mislead you, even if their wisdom might seem strange to your still job-addled mind.

Whereas The Plan is supposed to provide a simple means to a desirable end, for Josh, Jean, and Sherri the process of recovery had become an end in itself. Josh and Jean would constantly tell me how World Wide's books and advice had enriched their marriage and helped them to communicate with each other (the bolstering of marriage and family is a major theme in Amway). The Amway lore is also full of distributors, perhaps abused as children, who "couldn't even look people in the eye" when they joined, but who were now confidently showing The Plan to all and sundry.

Dreambuilders' impact on Sherri's life was far less salutary. Its most tangible financial effect was the used car she had bought with Josh's advice, which came complete with a weird smell and a glove compartment that didn't close. But Sherri felt that she had undergone a profound psychic transformation. "Before Amway," she would say, "I just wasn't *thinking*!" Her new clarity made her scornful of mass pursuits: When the E2020 staff went to a Cubs game, she could hardly believe that people would waste their time that way. (Josh counseled her to just sit next to strangers and *mingle*.) Her "j-o-b," even with a promotion to

Internet Expert, certainly didn't interest her anymore: She wanted to spend the whole day talking about The Business.[14] And she now regarded unambitious co-workers, family, and friends as, in Scott Coon's words, "slugs."

Her alienation didn't stop with non-Amwayers. She was also bitterly resentful of "crosslines," her Amway cousins who belonged to other downlines. As fellow unrecovered wage junkies, they were a potential reservoir of misinformation, discontent and backsliding. Josh cautioned her against fraternizing: Polite small talk was O.K., but you shouldn't, say, go to a movie with them (Amway lore is full of disaster stories about crosslines who carpool). But Sherri's animus went further. Crosslines were her competition, soaking up prospects and "saturating" Chicago before she had a chance. She was incensed when they hogged seats at meetings, hysterical when they went Direct.

As her world shrunk, she immersed herself in World Wide culture. For entertainment, she listened to the motivational tapes, laughing and crying at the tales of hardship and triumph. She read the WWDB recommended books, memorizing snippets of Norman Vincent Peale and *Psychocybernetics*. She urged me, likewise, to move to the "next level": to hook into Amvox voicemail (where I could listen to messages from my distant upline Greg Duncan courtside at Bulls-Magic games[15]); make plane and hotel reservations for the upcoming Family Reunion; and get on "standing order" to automatically receive six World Wide cassettes a month at six bucks a pop—which Josh claimed simply covered costs—presumably of meetings recorded onto very cheap tapes. ("I'd gladly pay more for them," Josh insisted, "because they're helping me to become financially liberated!") Sherri told me, in hushed tones, that "Greg Duncan judges you more on the number of standing orders in your downline than on your PV!" I didn't doubt it. The upper echelons of World-Wide and other groups rake in enormous profits from their speaking engagements and the sale of motivational materials. Dexter Yager, head of the Yager Group, is reputed to make more from his propaganda syndicate than from his actual Amway business.

While the whirlwind of meetings and events were great for cultivating denial, they seemed to do little to help distributors develop "strong and profitable businesses." Nor were they much good for attracting new blood into The Business. With the exception of First Looks, their extreme cultishness was distinctly off-putting to newcomers. Still, Josh, Jean, and Sherri continued to make the mistake of indiscriminately taking prospects to whatever meeting was going on. Even a Second Look (described ominously as more "motivational" and less informational than a First Look) was inadvisable for outsiders, as Sherri discovered when she

took her friend Elizabeth to one.

The car ride to the meeting went swimmingly. When Sherri mentioned job insecurity and the need to "diversify," Elizabeth couldn't have agreed more. When Sherri mentioned the time-money trap, Elizabeth knew just what she was talking about. A First Look might have had a real impact.

She was clearly expecting some sort of business seminar. (Sherri hadn't mentioned Amway and also cautioned me against doing so: "I've found that when I say 'Amway,' people get all . . ." she said, miming "running-away-screaming.") What Elizabeth got, however, was closer to a Pentecostal revival meeting. The featured speaker, Executive Diamond Brad Duncan (Greg's younger brother), was more Billy Sunday than financial analyst; he yelled, joked, screamed, and sermonized past the audience at "sinners" who pretended they didn't want to be rich and who dumped on anyone with ambition. He exhorted us to stop listening to our "broke" friends and relatives and allow ourselves to be influenced by successful millionaires: "I believe in the *power of association!*"

Brad spoke in parables: There was Brad's father-in-law, who, upon being given a brand-new souped-up truck, sat down and wept. After a few years, the "newness wore off," so Brad again bought him the latest model. And again his father-in-law sat down and wept. (Brad's own fluid dynamics were more spectacular: When he first saw the jazzed-up truck, he admitted, "urine streamed down" his pant legs.)

I was sitting next to Elizabeth and couldn't imagine what she was thinking. (True to form, Brad didn't mention Amway for over an hour.) At first, she laughed and clapped with the rest of the audience; as the evening wore on, however, there was a lag. Her responses became more tentative as the crowd of hundreds became more wildly, footstompingly enthusiastic. Afterwards, she was dazed and holloweyed. In the parking lot, Josh, Jean, and Sherri encircled her, urging her to meet with them the next day to learn more about The Business. Cornered, she agreed. After a few minutes in the car with Sherri, however, she regained enough strength to put the meeting off to the indefinite future. (Months later, she was still on Josh's "hopeful" list.)

Disappointments like this got Sherri down, and keeping her outlook positive was beginning to strain even World Wide Dreambuilders, LLC. At one First Look, Dave Duncan (Greg and Brad's father, a straight-talkin' Montanan who had given up a successful construction business to build dreams with Amway) reassured her with a timeline he drew on the eraser-board showing that you could make millions within 10 years. Afterwards, however, during the mingling— while Dave warned a young couple that, sure, some brain surgeons did well, but only the ones at the top— Sherri started eyeing the evening's hosts with despair. They were crosslines, Direct Distributors who had broken 7,500 PV with an all-out one-summer campaign. Sherri, almost beside herself, insisted that Josh, Jean, and I have a meeting to "figure out what we're going to do. Because we've got to do *something!*"

Josh also showed signs of breakdown. After the presentation he took his customary position near the speaker, a hand-held recorder jutting provocatively from his hip; but because he wasn't in Dave's downline, he wouldn't be able to accompany him to dinner. Josh claimed that it was at such dinners that speakers, unfettered by FTC restrictions, could reveal "the good stuff." He proposed tailing Dave to the restaurant: "They couldn't stop us, could they?" When Jean talked him out of this, he became desperate to simply "go somewhere and meet people." Jean reminded him it was a school night for her. "Well,

maybe we should talk to the hotel staff," he suggested.

My uplines' despair made me reluctant to add to their failure. But I had stayed in too long already. Having run out of other things to buy, I had resorted to subjecting my cat to Amway pet food. And I began to sense that when Josh and Sherri looked at me, they—in their last-ditch hopes— saw Diamonds. Before I disappeared from their lives, however, I accompanied them to one last Rally.

Rallies begin with a ritual called "crossing the stage," in which distributors who have attained a new bonus level go up to receive their commemorative pin and shake hands with a Diamond. From the crowd of about 500, two couples "crossed" at the 1,000 PV level (the lowest warranting a pin) and received a standing ovation

from the audience. From the stage, the host then called out all the levels from 1,500 PV to 7,500 PV. Nobody emerged from the audience—which, nonetheless, remained on its feet applauding. The host kept cajoling, "C'mon, there's plenty of room up here," as if it were shyness that was keeping people away. It was the archetypal Amway moment: a crowd giving a standing ovation to nobody.

The centerpiece of any Rally is the life-story told by the guest of honor, emphasizing the depths of his pre-Amway rut and his resurrection through The Business. That evening's featured guest, Executive Diamond Bill Hawkins, however, was too arrogant even to feign the requisite humility in his testimonial. He had been great all his life: a talented musician in one of Minneapolis' best bands, a brilliant school teacher, a voracious reader, a charming companion with hundreds of loyal friends, and an unbelievably prodigious drinker of beer (about which he was now "ashamed"). When he saw The Plan and realized that he was much smarter than the guy showing it, he knew that his ship had finally come in: Here, at last, was something that would adequately reward his greatness.[16]

Bill was one of the two types you find in Amway: the talented mountebank who knew a good hunting ground when he saw one. Confident in his superiority, he didn't need Amway to work for everybody, but didn't shy away from pretending that it would. Josh, Jean, and

Sherri, of course, represented the other type: the dupes.

To Bill, dupes would always be dupes, and he signaled his confidence in this by launching into a monologue that would have caused a scandal before a more critical audience. He told us, matter of factly, that World Wide had $8 million in assets, in which only those at the Diamond level had any equity; that the 20 World Widers who sat on its board frequently had food fights that splattered the HQ's silk wallpaper; and that World Wide tapes are so bad that Bill himself would regularly throw them out his car window. In short, he was tossing us rope to hang him with, baldly acknowledging that World Wide was nothing but a support system for a bunch of fast-talkers who lived high on the hog by charging their bamboozled underlings outrageous prices for spurious advice. This was the most damning critique of Amway I had ever heard. Yet none of it mattered to the crowd; they seemed only to be dreaming of the fancy wallpaper that they might one day be able to soil.

He ended with a *Wizard of Oz* motif, reminding us to stay positive and focused: "You have to stick to that yellow brick road. Just like Dorothy. She followed it all the way to the Emerald City—and picked up three legs along the way! You know what? *The Wizard of Oz* is really an Amway movie!" The crowd erupted in laughter and cheers. In the midst of their long applause, they seemed to have forgotten what the Wizard turned out to be.

Notes

[1] The FTC's ruling that Amway is not a pyramid scheme is based partly on the "70-10 Rule": To qualify for Performance Bonuses based on downlines' sales, an Amway distributor is required to sell, according to Amway's *Business Reference Manual*, "at wholesale and/or retail at least 70 percent of the total amount of products he bought during a given month"—this is supposed to prevent "inventory loading," the forced purchase of unsalable merchandise. Amwayers are also required, for the Performance Bonus, to sell to at least ten retail customers in a given month, which ensures that real business is being conducted.

Both parts of the 70-10 Rule have major loopholes. According to the *Business Reference Manual*, "for purposes of [the 70 Percent Rule], products used for personal or family consumption or given out as samples are also considered as part of sales volume." Thus, overbuying for "personal use" is not ruled out. As for the Ten-Customer Rule, the *Manual* states that the "distributor should not disclose the prices at which he or she made the ten retail sales." This makes possible a practice alluded to by a World Wide speaker: giving Amway products away to ten people and calling them "retail sales." He added that the income from the Performance Bonus made the giveaways well worth it.

The FTC also cites Amway's "Buyback Rule" as a feature distiguishing the Business from a pyramid scheme. Distributors can return any "products, literature, or sales aids" for "whatever refund is agreed upon between the departing distributor and his or her sponsor." The *Manual* adds this note: "To return Amway literature for credit or refund, the literature must be sent back in its original wrapping, unopened and unused."

[2] Nowadays, nearly all Amwayers identify with a "distributor group." Dream Night, in fact, was arranged not by Amway, but by World Wide Dreambuilders LLC, which is constituted by the downlines of Crown Ambassador Bill Britt. These groups, which do the heavy lifting of building and inspiring downlines, have no legal connection to Amway (as indicated by the disclaimers on the back of tickets for Dream Night and every other World Wide function I attended: "This event is produced and offered independently of Amway Corporation and has not been reviewed or endorsed by Amway"). The corporation uses the legal independence of distributor groups to its advantage. In a class-action lawsuit brought by former Amwayers charging Amway Corporation, World Wide head Bill Britt, and Dexter Yager with fraud and price-fixing, Amway claimed that it was itself, in effect, a victim of Britt and Yager's tactics—and thus not liable. (The case has since been settled out of court.)

Having repudiated Britt and Yager, Amway promptly welcomed them back into the fold: Both recently made the cover of Amway's in-house magazine, *Amagram*, and Yager received the Founders Distinguished Service Award.

[3] The names Sherri, Josh, and Jean are pseudonyms.

[4] As soon as they mention Amway, First Look speakers always hurry to dispel "myths" about The Business: that it's a rinky-dink soap company, that it requires door-to-door sales, that it's a pyramid scheme (if you draw an organizational chart of a typical corporation, guess what, that *looks* like a pyramid too!), that you have to be a Christian to join (there's nobody The Business wouldn't accept), that it's a crazy cult (Amway provides an opportunity to everybody, meaning that it inevitably lets in some bad apples who damage its reputation).

[5] This wasn't exactly true: The bonus is calculated on the basis of sales of 100 "PV" a month; PV, or Point Value, is a play currency that converts to American legal tender at a rate of about 1 to 3.5. Each distributor in one's pyramid would have to spend around $350 a month in real money to generate the $2,000 bonus.

[6] Once, when we had arrived at the wrong Holiday Inn for a World Wide meeting—right interstate, wrong unincorporated area—Josh wrung some victory out of defeat by coming up with a "great ice-breaker" to use on the lone airline pilot in the lobby: "You're with United? You must be *friendly!*"

[7] A "Direct Distributor" is one whose group does 7,500 PV or more in monthly sales (which is almost $25,000 a month in U.S. currency, a far more daunting figure which the artificial PV currency helps to disguise). Direct Distributors are entitled to order directly from Amway without going through their upline sponsor, as the lower ranks must do. Once you are a Direct Distributor, your group is no longer nested in your sponsor's. From then on your sponsor gets only a straight 4 percent cut (the "Leadership Bonus") of your group's sales. You accrue more bonuses by lining up DDs under your direct sponsorship: six DDs make you a Diamond, twelve a Double Diamond, twenty a Crown Ambassador.

[8] To be fair, the *Amagram* occasionally has a "Catalog Sale" section, where a handful of items are offered at discounts.

[9] The Amway *Business Reference Manual* itself gives the lie to the 30 percent figure. It calculates the Basic Discount by subtracting a product's wholesale distributor cost from the suggested retail price (both denominated in dollars) and then dividing them by the BV price, which is set by Amway for each product but which is usually smaller than the U.S. dollar

price. If the calculation is done *solely* in dollars, the Basic Discount shrinks to about 17 percent. And when I did a real price comparison, that 17 percent came down to about 4 percent.

[10] Not that there aren't limits. The food in Amway leans heavily toward the pricey, overpackaged "meal kit" and portable "nutrition bar." Woe to those who try to buy a bag of rice through The Business—not to mention fresh produce or meat, though you *can* have frozen steaks air-mailed to you.

[11] At the top, the multi-multi's seem to attain a Zen of conspicuous consumption. Brad Duncan, brother of the great Double Diamond Greg Duncan, described seeing a dusty Rolls Royce among the many cars in the garage of his upline mentor, Ron Puryear; when he asked what he paid for it, Ron answered, "I don't know. Whatever the sticker price was." Brad took him to task for this, until Ron lectured: "That dealership is somebody's livelihood—somebody with a family. I'm not so hard up that I need to haggle the food out of a child's mouth." Brad was chastened, realizing that only small minds pay attention to sticker prices.

[12] Amway gives some idea of real chances for success in its "Amway Business Review" pamphlet, which the FTC requires it provide to all prospects. The "Business Review" is an ingenious mixture of mandated honesty and obfuscatory spin: The average monthly gross income for "active" distributors, for instance, is revealed to be a meager $65 a month; but the "Review" leaves out the *median* income and the *net* profit, both of which would probably be negative. Likewise, it states that "2 percent of all 'active' distributors who sponsor others and approximately 1 percent of all 'active' distributors met Direct Distributor qualification requirements during the survey period." From this, it derives the optimistic conclusion that "once again, the survey demonstrates a substantial increase in achievement for those who share the business with others." *Increase* implies that there are some non-sharing distributors who succeed; an alternate reading of the statistics would be that all distributors *try* to share, none succeed *without* sharing, but only half are *able to share*. It's also a measure of Amway's PR savvy that every article I've seen (even the critical ones) that mentions the number of Directs uses the 2 percent, rather than the more accurate 1 percent, figure.

[13] The recovery slant also solves a troubling logical conundrum for Amwayers. On the one hand, Amwayers are utterly dependent on job holders—not only to manufacture and transport their products, but to provide them with clerical assistance when they're Diamonds (Greg Duncan boasted of the size of his staff, which does his actual distribution work) and, above all, make their millions worth something in the outside economy. But on the other hand, Amway is supposed to offer a sure-fire alternative to wage labor. What will keep all of the essential workers from becoming distributors? The answer lies in weakness of the flesh: Just as there will always be alcoholics, junkies, and overeaters, so there will always be many people without the resolve or courage to join Amway.

[14] I got the impression that she was becoming a laughingstock at work, an experience common enough to have spawned a whole genre of revenge fantasies in the Amway lore. Speakers always describe the retirement party you'll be able to throw for yourself, complete with fireworks, to really stick it to the naysayers who once laughed at you. They also describe the houses and vacations you'll give to your parents, who'll finally realize how wrong they were about The Business. The yearning to save face—especially with people you urged to join Amway—seems to be a major factor keeping people in.

[15] Rich DeVos owns the Orlando Magic basketball team, which allows Amway to use Shaquille O'Neal's name for their "Shaq Bars," treats which taste like chaff stuck together with heavy-duty honey-flavored adhesive. When I reluctantly ate one at a meeting, a passing World Wider commented, "I *love* those. You need to eat them with a *lot* of water, though."

[16] His tedious auto-encomium was enlivened only by occasional, chilling anecdotes of violence: His mother hit him as a child until, old and strong enough, he could credibly threaten to hit her back; his frat brothers, drunken and rambunctious, tried to shave his head one night, whereupon he barricaded himself in his room, audibly cocked a semiautomatic shotgun, and threatened to kill them; and his family needled him about Amway until, one Thanksgiving, he jumped up and shouted, "I don't dump on what you do, and if you keep dumping on what I do, I'll take you outside and knock your block off; and if you're a woman, I don't know what I'll do!"

2
SUB-CONTRACT THE JOB

from **Aurora**

THOMAS GEOGHEGAN

CHICAGO, *1989. A strike that has been going on for some time has finally collapsed. The union is facing ruination and the company has filed suit for millions in damages. On the eve of the trial,* GIL, *the union's lawyer, stumbles into a romantic triangle between his North Side ex-fiancée and the union leader's South Side daughter. Unwitting of her daughterhood, he has asked* ANN, *only 23, on a date.*

Scene: The North Avenue Beach.
GIL *and* ANN *are at the water's edge.*

ANN: *(twirls around)* How could you be so cool as to take me to Hubbard Street?

GIL: You, uh, like, dance?

ANN: Like it? Oh, yes! That's why I like this city . . . . It's so flat, perfect to dance on.

GIL: Perfect to land on . . . that's all it's good for, isn't it? Just a big place, for an airport . . . .

ANN: Oh, no!

GIL: Only I can't escape. I feel like I'm stranded.

ANN: *(mocking)* But what about by sea? Look at all the little boats, baby boats . . . .

GIL: Oh, yes, poor baby boats, little baby white wine, they're trapped here too . . . . But you like it, huh? Lately I've begun to wonder, "Do women really like the Midwest?"

ANN: We like Marshall Field's.

GIL: I have a friend, a woman, she says we ought to take a knife and divide up the country, sexually . . . the women'd get the coasts, the men'd get the middle . . . .

ANN: *(shocked)* Take . . . a knife, and . . . cut off the men's middle?

GIL: No, it's . . . *(pause)* No . . . you know . . . I don't even know your last name.

ANN: *(groans)* This is like the South Side! "What *was* her last name?" *(burrows in purse)* Hey, want to see my I.D.?

GIL: No, no . . . .

ANN: No, I'll take my finger and just write it in the sand . . . .

GIL: Oh! Don't put your finger—

ANN: *(looks up)* Why?

GIL: *(shivers)* It's full of lead, asbestos—

ANN: Oh, no, see? It's just sand, like up in Michigan! But I turn around and there's the Sears!

GIL: When I see the city, like tonight, the turrets, and music boxes, and minarets, it's aglow, it's like on fire, like a burning bush . . . . I want to take off my shoes, like I'm standing on holy ground.

ANN: Good! Let's take off our shoes . . . . *(She flips hers off.)*

GIL: *(aghast)* What are you doing?

ANN: *(sets them down)* You don't do this on first dates?

GIL: Oh, Ann . . . . I have to say . . . when we came out of the theater, the way you took off your socks, and gave 'em to the beggar . . . .

ANN: I didn't have any change, I thought, "Oh, give him something." *(now writes name with toe.)*

GIL: I mean, he's wearing them . . . your socks! *(pause)* Oh no, you'll get asbestos . . . .

ANN: *(still writing)* Sorry, kind of a hard name . . . . But you don't like Chicago?

GIL: Oh, most of the old Chicago is so empty now. Empty Goldblatt's, empty el cars at night, headed the wrong way . . . Even the lake, here, looks a bit empty. Look, the damn thing doesn't even gurgle.

ANN: It's resting. *(fondly, to the lake)* Oh, it's such a dear.

GIL: *(coming to see what she wrote)* Can I read this? "G-E-R" . . . "G" . . . oh, "Y," oh why? *(slaps head)* Why me! Why? *(to* ANN*)* You! You're D-D's . . . his daughter!

ANN: I had to laugh when you came up to me on the el . . . . *(laughs)* Good thing I gave you my phone at work!

GIL: Laugh? Oh shit!

ANN: Oh so what? So we went on a little date. . . .

GIL: This very night, your dad, he begged me, "Come to the hall," and here I am, up on the North Side, *ab-ducing* his daughter!

ANN: Is it true what my father says? How can you leave us?

GIL: *(groans)* I'm trapped . . . . Look, I . . . .

ANN: You think the strike was wrong? My father, all these men, should have taken all those wage cuts. . . . Eight dollars an hour for the people my age? My father says, "Our fathers, our grandfathers, fought for those things . . . we have no right to give them up!"

GIL: Maybe we should have given them up, anyway!

ANN: But didn't you say that, too, down at the hall one night, "We have to fight back"?

GIL: I said that? Oh stop it . . . *(He picks up sand, lets it run through fingers.)* See? "Sand like up in Michigan!" I feel, these men, like I've led them into the desert, led them here to die.

ANN: Don't give up! But how did all this happen anyway? Is it because . . . all the people without shoes in the Third World, with all their low wages?

GIL: Oh no, that's not it.

ANN: Well, then, what happened? I'm 23, nobody tells me.

GIL: People your age don't really know. . . . Well, it's simple: You don't have the right, under American law, to join a union.

ANN: Prove it.

GIL: O.K., you work for me, right?

ANN: *(salutes)* Right!

GIL: You put on a union button.

ANN: Hurray!

GIL: You're fired!

ANN: I'll file a complaint!

GIL: O.K., but it'll take four years. . . .

ANN: Aaah! Four years?

GIL: First the Ad Law Judge, that's two years . . . then the full board in D.C., that's another year. . . . O.K., but you win. *Win.* So, do I have to take you back?

ANN: Yes!

GIL: No! Now you have to file a case in a court . . . not a little court either, but a big court . . . U.S. Court of Appeals . . . three guys in black dresses who sit around reading Ayn Rand . . . But O.K., O.K., let's say you finally win. Now do I owe you money?

ANN: Yes!

GIL: No! Because you got a job, like, at Fresh Fields. I don't owe you anything. In fact, at my place, I'm now paying a wage even lower than at Fresh Fields.

ANN: I want to come back anyway!

GIL: Yeah? Well, I warn you . . . better not!

ANN: No, I'm back! Just to spite you.

GIL: Fine. Welcome back. You're fired.

ANN: I have to go through all this again?

GIL: *(looks at watch)* See you back here in four years.

ANN: No wonder why we're the only union left!

GIL: That's why they're just going house to house now, like in World War II, shooting people like your father.

ANN: What can we do?

GIL: Just stand right here on the beach and watch the city burn.

ANN: *(shrugs, steps off stage)* After what you said . . . I feel safer stepping out in the water.

GIL: *(gapes at her)* It's . . . freezing . . . isn't it?

ANN: Oh well, I'm a real Trojan!

GIL: Spartan?

ANN: *(mocking)* Whatever! You're one too! Still standing there on all that sand. All that sand, it's full of lead and asbestos. . . .

GIL: *(looks down)* Well, maybe I'll just put a foot in. . . .

ANN: Come on!

GIL: God it's cold!

ANN: *(cups her hands, full of lake)* Here, take the chill off . . . take a little sip. . . .

GIL: "Take a little sip"? Are you out of your mind?

ANN: *(she sips)* Do this every day, mmm-mmm . . . guess what happens?

GIL: *(edgy)* What?

ANN: You'll get polio! No, no, I'm only kidding . . . here, sip!

GIL: Absolutely not!

ANN: Oh! Watch out for that wave!

GIL: What? *(A wave falls, vertically, and douses GIL)* I'm wet. I'm in Lake Michigan. And I'm wet.

ANN: *(laughing)* We're soaked.

GIL: Do I need a tetanus shot? *(licks his lips)* My God . . .

ANN: What?

GIL: It tastes like . . . beer, like really lousy lite beer.

ANN: You didn't know?

GIL: You mean those pumping stations?

ANN: *(delighted)* They're breweries! *(A second wave falls, douses them.)*

GIL: Oh shit!

ANN: *(splutters)* The lake is mad . . . cause you said it didn't even gurgle!

GIL: *(licks his arm)* Hell . . . maybe

we should fight back, I mean . . .
a little . . . not too much, just a
little. . . .

ANN: I knew you'd say that if you
got out here. . . .

GIL: I do feel better . . . no, I do . . . I
love to look up at the stars . . . .

ANN: *(closer to him)* You do?

GIL: You know about the Big Bang?

ANN: No, I went to DePaul.

GIL: *(dreamy)* I was in it, you were
in it, Daniel Barenboim playing
Bach was in it . . . all the Bach
partitas came out of the Big
Bang!

ANN: I wish I'd known you then.

GIL: Oh, but you and I . . . it's not
. . . *(moving back, nervous)* I . . .

I was born in the decade they
had World War II. . . .

ANN: You weren't in it, were you?

GIL: No, I was in the sixties.

ANN: *(purrs)* So braaave. . . .

GIL: *(nervous)* Oh, don't you see?
You're my . . . my . . . daughter's
client . . . and . . . *(as Ann moves
closer)* a lawyer should avoid
even the ap-p-pearance of incest . . . .

ANN: *(touching him)* Can I ask you
something?

GIL: What?

ANN: Did you think, back in the Big
Bang, we were going to date?

*(A kiss: Third wave crashes
down.)*

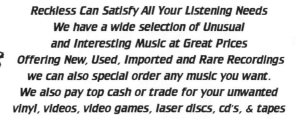

Event

to be happy
to be afraid
to flee
the atmosphere is metaphysical

to be sad
to stop
to dash joyfully
to reverse
the future is anatomical

reversed
combined
solidified

its
its or
its are
the all is fantasy

(*damn* Miss Tickle!)

—Keith Waldrop

Boom Crash Opera
Shadow-Boxing in the Culture Bubble

CHRIS LEHMANN

"FROM every corner of the earth where the unfettered industrial system was grinding out the raw materials for wealth, crushing men's bones, parching their blood, following them in a perpetual orgy of chicane and debauchery, came the onrushing flood of pennies pilfered from the poor, from the ignorant and from the savages, from indentured slaves who treaded the death mill to beat a rhythm to the saturnalia of America's unbridled profits."

Thus did Kansas Republican and one-time Hoover man William Allen White recall the great bull market that lifted off in 1927 and crashed rather unceremoniously two years later. True, White, one of the decade's great reformers and journalists, had always kept a certain moral and political loyalty to his political coming-of-age during the Progressive era, but it's nonetheless striking to ponder how peremptorily the business boosterism of the 1920s curdled into rhetoric that might well have made Marx himself blush. White delivered his thunderous judgment, by the way, not in some street-corner anarchist tract, but in a sympathetic politi-cal biography of President Calvin Coolidge, the stiff New Englander who silently fidgeted while the economic order burned.

Now, of course, we have pretty much banished the thought of White's death mill and its tenders, and we congratulate ourselves that we would never have the bad taste, if we were to remember them, to do so with such pejorative terms as "ignorant" and "savages." Indeed, the whole industrial system has, in the popular mind, been magically effaced, and the historical table reset with the goblets and aliments of Information Age capitalism. Wealth is now created in suburban office parks, pleasantly minded by the Dockers-clad geeks and engineers who preside over the end of history. Who, after all, could picture awshucks Microsoft supremo Bill Gates in an orgy of chicane and debauchery?

However, the unquiet shade of the twenties is not staying put. Its shimmering surface—that high old time of flappers, speakeasies, hopheads, and jazz fanciers—exerts a continuing fascination among our keepers of the zeitgeist. Nostalgic cable channels program "1920s weeks" and ads for Beefeater gin taunt, "There was a decade called the Roaring Twenties. What will yours be called?"

Happy Days Are Where, Again?

BUT it's in the field of economic prognostication that the twenties have their most persistent cachet. In a recent cover story on "The New Rich," *Newsweek* christened our own purblind time of greed and info-idolatry "the Roaring Nineties" and confidently declared that the bull market is "making instant billionaires—and changing America." Of course, *Newsweek*'s frantic bandwagon-hopping raises certain suspicions about its own grasp of history: It was only last year, after all, that the magazine ran a downsizing cover with the crypto-Buchananite headline "corporate killers"—and it would obviously be too much for the zeitgeist-happy *Newsweek* brain trust to pause and reflect that the new ranks of "Microsoft millionaires" have seen their investor returns skyrocket thanks to the killing sprees of downsizing CEOs.

Newsweek, in any event, only brings up the rear of the sanguine permaboom parade. In fact, the financial press has been boosting the inviting tableau of unruffled, perpetual prosperity since the current bull market took off in 1995. And of course the most blinding reveries of pelf ascendant come from that tireless exponent of Information Age capitalism, *Wired* maga-zine. *Wired*'s massive July cover story plumbs "The Long Boom," a conceit hatched by *Wired* features editor Peter Leyden and Peter Schwartz, doyen of the Global Business Network—a visionary think tank of the digiterati that boasts among its members such cyberseers as Stewart Brand, William Gibson, Laurie Anderson, and Brian Eno.

The countless cracked details of the Schwartz and Leyden scenario don't bear repeating. Mainly, "The Long Boom" is a wish list for an info-imperium, a society in which all sectors of life cop the same techno-buzz and spontaneously do things like devise "a new information-age standard of measuring economic growth" and "begin to shift from hierarchical processes to networked ones." Imagine *Newsweek*'s own feel-good economic columnist Robert Samuelson drooling over his fortieth bong hit, and you begin to get the picture.

"Building a digital civilization" is, indeed, *Wired*'s new unofficial slogan, its former task of shepherding

Who Remembers the Depression?

40 years and older in 1930	𝕏𝕏𝕏
30-39 years in 1930	𝕏𝕏𝕏
20-29 years in 1930	𝕏𝕏𝕏𝕏
10-19 years in 1930	𝕏𝕏𝕏𝕏𝕏
Under 10 years in 1930	𝕏𝕏𝕏𝕏𝕏
Not born in 1930	𝕏𝕏𝕏𝕏𝕏𝕏𝕏𝕏𝕏𝕏𝕏𝕏𝕏𝕏𝕏𝕏

Each figure represents 5 million people in the 1955 population of the U.S.

the "digital revolution" into being evidently a fait accompli. You'd think that a company that has twice failed to mount a credible IPO in today's overheated stock market might have other worries than launching a global *mission civilatrice*. But daft as it is, this clamor over civilization and communications technology claims a wide cultural ambit in contemporary America: House Speaker Newt Gingrich has nattered tirelessly on the inestimable virtues of "American civilization," the mandate to spread it indiscriminately and the grave threats that Great Society social engineering poses to it. And of course, techno-utopianism is rife in every nook and cranny of American commerce and culture. Indeed, Schwartz and Leyden might as well have cribbed the title of their Long Boom manifesto from MCI's current Internet ad campaign: "Is this a great time, or what?"

Here, in fact, the notion of a resurgent twenties culture starts to get rather interesting. We can blow a salutary shotgun out of Schwartz and Leyden's history bong by noting that the twenties were much obsessed with parallel questions of communication and civilization, even as they were steeped in equally foolish prophecies of a permanent prosperity.

Where do such preoccupations come from? One likely source is a striking, and feverishly repressed, instability in the distribution of the largesse kicked up in the wake of great speculative booms. In economic terms, no recent era in American history bears a greater resemblance to our own than the

twenties does, mixing runaway growth in the paper economy with ever-steepening social inequality underneath.

The Culture Sublimation

Yet then, as now, few Americans were greatly exercised over, or even aware of, the downward ratcheting of the citizenry's comparative economic advantage. Instead, they clamored—then, as now—about crises of cultural self-definition. The "great fear" of the twenties, historian Warren Susman writes, was "whether any great industrial and democratic mass society can maintain a significant level of civilization, and whether mass education and mass communication will allow any civilization to survive." Strewn atop the squalor of the era's inequality, in other words, was the elastic scrim of culture, beneath which the unaddressed issues of the day got rearranged into various grand and unedifying questions of civilization's destiny.

Indeed, as Susman argues, the era developed a certain Hegelian mania for fusing the talismans of civilization atop the sprawling infrastructures of communications. Hence the mad rush to catalogue and popularize most fields of knowledge, chiefly through imposing tomes such as H.G. Wells's *Outline of History*; the reverent Art Deco palaces erected as monuments to the mass-disseminated miracles of the motion picture and the automobile; the fevered excitement of intellectuals over the modernist dispensation, captured, for example, in the lapsed preacher Vachel

Lindsay's celebration of America's new "hieroglyphic civilization."

But such questions of cultural-cum-civilizational meaning permeated far beyond the keepers of higher culture and practitioners of high modernism who people Susman's argument. The twenties were in fact every bit as much a decade of runaway popular *Kulturkampf* as they were an era of thinly distributed prosperity. Indeed, we can say that the decade inaugurated an arresting leitmotif in modern American history. Call it the Culture Bubble: the inflation of the terms of cultural debate as conditions of social inequality teeter on the brink of intolerability.

Cultural conflict is at least as old as the American republic, as any cursory look at Puritan election-day sermons will quickly confirm. Yet in their modern-to-postmodern incarnation, the Culture Wars—the paint-by-numbers ritual in which the warring parties trade accusations of depravity, repression, and historical obsolescence, with the state usually conscripted to referee—made their bones in the twenties. Fundamentalists railed against evolution; eugenicists, Klansmen, and patrician pseudoscientists inveighed against runaway immigration and racial mongrelizing; the Wilsonian apostles of civilized uplift conspired with the heavily feminized ranks of religious crusaders to produce Prohibition; less genteel official reactionaries weighed in with still cruder measures of sociopolitical control, such as the Palmer raids against foreign-born radicals and stalwart employer-friendly campaigns against union organizing; the

New Woman and the Lost Generation marked the first appearance of the twentieth century's Great Amoral Youth Question; jazz, radio, and the popular cinema all furnished incontrovertible evidence to scores of bush-league Spenglers that the long slide into barbarism was under way; the growth of the automobile, modern advertising and a commercialized mass culture erased the incorrigible regionalism and parochialism of America's rural village life, prompting intellectuals such as Sinclair Lewis and Robert and Helen Lynd into fervid denunciations of small-town homogeneity and lodge-brother groupthink.

One could go through this litany and glibly substitute latter-day civilizing themes and culture crusades into the templates the twenties left behind: The war on drugs and anti-smoking hysteria for Prohibition; the V-chip for the Hays Code; *The Bell Curve* for Madison Grant's *Perils of the Great Race*; Generation X for the Lost Generation; *Fargo* for *Main Street*; Buchananite immigration hysteria for Klan-led immigration hysteria; and fundamentalism for, well, fundamentalism. Yet such one-to-one correspondences only elide the key, broader point regarding the Culture Bubble: These elaborate contretemps over the culture's robustness and behavior-policing efficacy are rarely about the country's real troubles or much of anything at all. Indeed, they furnish the compass by which the embarrassing, discomfiting matters of social class can be endlessly skirted.

This point can be nailed down, with reference both to that distant

Roaring time and our own present one, with a few bracing statistics. Surveying the economic changes wrought during the twenties, historian Robert McElvaine notes that as the decade ended, 0.1 percent of the population—some 24,000 families—enjoyed an income equivalent to that of 42 percent of the American population—or 11.2 million families. From 1920 to 1929, aggregate American disposable income rose by 9 percent, while among the top 1 percent of the population it rose by 75 percent—from 12 percent of the nation's total in 1920 to 19 percent in 1929. The distribution of wealth—stocks, equity, and savings—was even more upwardly skewed. By 1929, the top 0.5 percent of the population controlled 32.4 percent of individual net wealth in America—the highest such concentration in American history.

Until now, anyway. Even though all the returns aren't in from the current bull market—which will only accelerate current trends—all the indications suggest, as *Business Week* economists William Wolman and Anne Colamosca argue, that the nineties have "witnessed a concentration of wealth that is without historical precedent in the United States," making the upward consolidation of wealth in the twenties "only a pallid prelude." Between 1983 and 1992, the top 1 percent of Americans increased their net wealth by a whopping 28.3 percent; in the same period median wealth declined by 8.1 percent, and the bottom 40 percent of the population lost 49.7 percent of its net wealth.

The landscape of American enterprise in the nineties remains, despite its many new info-bells and whistles, a playground of unprosecuted leviathans and trusts. Just as Andrew Mellon (who played both sides of the street as an aluminum baron and the Harding-Coolidge Secretary of Treasury) has his nineties analog in Goldman Sachs don/Treasury boss Robert Rubin, so does Henry Ford, who lorded over the dominant growth industry of his day, beg comparisons with Bill Gates. Likewise, entire industries—from Gates's software empire to the merger-happy military, aerospace, media, and entertainment complexes—are effectively controlled by a handful of cartelized players, much as utilities, banking, and oil were 70-odd years ago.

Cartelization proves in all ages to be unquestionably good for business—or rather for the charmed circle of business owners. From

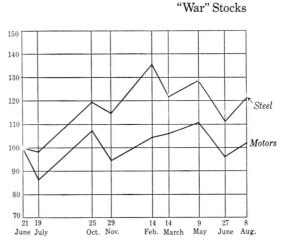

"War" Stocks

Steel

Motors

| | 21 June | 19 July | | 25 Oct. | 29 Nov. | | 14 Feb. | 14 March | 9 May | 27 June | 8 Aug. |

1923 to 1929, the income of workers inched up by 11 percent. That may look positively socialistic next to today's labor-soaking economic order—but only until one notes that over the same period corporate profits rose by a staggering 62 percent, and dividends shot up 65 percent. And while the book has yet to be closed on our own decade, this parallel, too, is unmistakable: The Economic Policy Institute notes that corporate profit rates took off in 1986, and have been rising steadily ever since. Nineteen ninety-six saw the greatest boost in the rate of both before- and after-tax corporate profits (11.39 percent and 7.57 percent, respectively) since record-keeping began in 1959.

Pretty Vacant

IT'S not hard to see why, in a social order as resolutely individualist as America's, these rather straightforward matters of distributive injustice get sublimated, as it were, into inherently insoluble matters of cultural identity. This isn't to say that all culture is reducible to material inequality, as the yeoman Marxist oversimplifications of base and superstructure blithely assume. But it is arresting to ponder the ways in which submerged grievances of class send American discourses of culture and morality into a curiously weightless kind of hyperspace.

In part, of course, social inequality makes only the most muffled peep amid the tumult of America's great cultural barbecue for quite obvious reasons. The myth of classlessness is the most reverently enshrined article of our social faith. There are no savagely truncated life opportunities or bitterly marginalized outcastes in American social mythology—only entrepreneurs waiting to happen. Thus popular discussions of poverty in America almost never engage the core questions of blighted, rapidly resegregating urban schools or industrial employers that gleefully decamp from urban neighborhoods for cut-rate labor markets in the developing world. Instead, they chase the ever-receding tails of the "culture of poverty" and underclass debates, which open obligingly onto the great question of how best to police the black family.

But critical distinctions between class and culture stubbornly elude us, since the inviolate logic of the Culture Bubble is, in many ways, the story of the past American Century: Time and again, steepening class polarization sends American public discourse a-dithering into queries over What It Means To Be An American. We seek to shore up the edifice of unfair life outcomes with the crumbling mortar of behavioral reform.

To help maintain this airtight state of denial, moreover, the news media willfully veer from any material touching on the public weal. Frederick Lewis Allen, one of the twenties' ablest chroniclers, writes that the era of Coolidge prosperity stands out in historical memory for "the unparalleled rapidity and unanimity with which millions of men and women turned their attention, their talk, and their emotional interest upon a series of tremendous trifles—a heavyweight boxing match, a murder trial, a new automobile model, a transatlantic flight." These interests were stirred, as it happens, by a media industry that, like its latter-day counterpart, was consolidating its institutional ranks as it multiplied its audience: The number of newspapers dropped from 2,580 in 1914 to 2,001 in 1926, as their readers shot up from 28 to 36 million. By 1927, 55 newspaper chains controlled 230 papers with a combined circulation of 13 million.

Today, as the income gap widens to an unprecedented scale, we have again watched the money culture modulate into so much celebrity planespotting. Global financial markets may shudder and once-secure, unionized workforces may spiral into temp and part-time limbo, but we worry that surly White Sox slugger Albert Belle may not be worth $55 million, that maybe Jim Carrey isn't hilarious enough to merit $20 million a picture, or that Elaine, Kramer, and company—our Seinfeld buddies— might be overpaid at $400,000 an episode. These celebrity glyphs allow us to formulate nonthreatening judgments on individual character—that Julia Louis-Dreyfus always seemed a little too stuck up, and didn't Jim Carrey ditch his first wife?— in lieu of asking whether it's patently delusional to imagine that eight-figure incomes can be "deserved" in the first place. Or, for that matter, asking just what the culture of celebritism is doing in the forefront of national consciousness.

Celebritism, indeed, provides a key reading of the Culture Bubble's progress. The degree to which questions of personality subsume substantive political debate roughly corresponds to our impatience with the more ponderous matters of social equity. In the early twenties the American farm economy was plunged into a decade-plus depression by the postwar boom in European credit and the concomitant deflation of commodity prices, but Washington stolidly hewed to the laissez-faire-mal line in deference to the stock market's keepers. The farm relief measures that managed to pass through Congress were dutifully vetoed by President Coolidge as intemperate meddling with the market. The consequences? Rural America's plight was magically distilled into H.L. Mencken and Sinclair Lewis' hectoring of the booboisie (and allied celebrations of the "civilized minority") or Klan/lodge-brother mobilizations of bigotry. The great symbolic clash between rural and urban civilization climaxed in 1925 with a stage-managed sociodrama in Dayton, Tennessee, where William

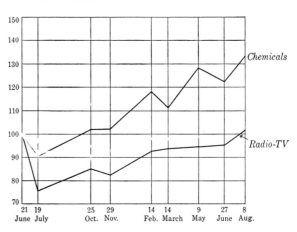

"Peace" Stocks

Jennings Bryan debated evolution on a courthouse lawn with big-city agnostic Clarence Darrow.

Now consider, in our own day, the many efficacious uses of celebritism for short-circuiting political debate. Why should we demand crackdowns on the new global sweatshop's sub-contractors, as long as Kathy Lee did enough damage control for her clothing line to start feeling perky again? Why should feminist writers agonize over comparable worth or daycare, when we've got Katie Roiphe, Naomi Wolf, and Karen Lehrman clamoring over the fine points of dating or "the lipstick proviso"? Few people today remember that 1992's great "Murphy Brown" flap was not merely a symbolic controversy over single motherhood, but Dan Quayle's official pronouncement on the causes of the L.A. riots. That the federal government's most sustained response to the second greatest civil disturbance in American history could be a fight picked with a television character speaks volumes about the suction power of the Culture Bubble. Candidate Bill Clinton made his own statement on race that same long, daft summer by picking a fight with a rap artist.

Five besotted years later, we don't find it at all unusual that our discussions of race are principally shaped by perceptions of a celebrity murder trial, that our first lady should chide a motion picture character for smoking on screen, that the scale of Bill Gates's estate commands more attention than the collapse of federal inner-city housing or that a princess who was evidently not versed in the operations of a seatbelt becomes a postmodern saint.

Enterprises such as *George* magazine are, of course, premised on the notion that celebrity culture and political discourse are identical—a claim it sought to demonstrate recently by publishing photos of its talentless avatar, JFK Jr., in the virtual buff. Meanwhile, in an entirely apt grace note to the forward march of celebritism, the only recent successful defense of liberalism in the marketplace of ideas was a book called *Rush Limbaugh Is a Big Fat Idiot*—penned, of course, by a TV personality.

The Right-to-Lifestyle Movement

BUT another coefficient of the Culture Bubble is a general exhaustion of political ideas. Every history of the decade notes that the charming, gregarious nitwit Warren Harding inadvertently christened the twenties a time of "normalcy," misreading the word "normality" in his inauguration speech. What is less widely noted is that the substance of the speech itself called for the burial of Progressivism, widely discredited as the liberal dogma of social experimentation that led to the catastrophe of the Great War. Rededicating the Republic to its historic "concern for preserved civilization," Harding warned that "our most dangerous tendency is to expect too much of government" and pronounced the mandate to keep wages and prices within their "normal balances." This meant trusting the "unmistakable" momentum of "the forward course of the business cycle" and, naturally, "the omission of unnecessary interference of Government with business" and "an end to Government's experiment in business." Harding's laconic successor Calvin Coolidge stopped all the flowery talk of civilization and cut to the chase, pronouncing redundantly that "the business of America is business."

In our age, of course, liberalism, rather than Progressivism, has become the great untouchable political doctrine, a bacillus to be vigilantly quarantined in the gleaming laboratory of global business civilization. Clinton's declaration in his 1995 State of the Union address that "the era of big government is over" was every bit the valentine to Wall Street—and confession of intellectual bankruptcy—that Coolidge's tautologies and Harding's paeans to civilized normalcy were in their day.

Clintonism has made good on the rhetoric of Government Lite, and not only through such blunt and unlovely means as the Personal Responsibility Act of 1996 (another nice touch, this—defenestrating federal entitlements to millions of impoverished mothers and children with disciplinary culturespeak about individual "responsibility"). Indeed, the Clinton era will likely be remembered as the time when government wandered around like a bored child on a rainy Saturday, dreaming up busywork to make itself feel like it was up to something important. Entire sectors of public life have been dumbed down into miniature culture crusades in increasingly flailing efforts to bulk up and define a postideological presidency. Education, in many ways the mother of all contemporary American inequali-

ties, is given the digital civilization treatment—glib national-standards rhetoric and millennial talk of VDTs on every desktop—as school infrastructure crumbles and urban districts hemorrhage away their tax bases. Racism is to be assuaged with official apologies and a national "conversation." Teen anomie is to be micromanaged with feelgood measures such as drivers' license drug tests and the V-chip. Citizens in need, in short, have become the moral equivalent of trick-or-treaters, dismissed at the door with paternal good wishes (or perhaps a lecture and an apology) and a fistful of morsels that will, likely as not, rot their teeth.

The forces of dissent, meanwhile, nicely fit the sobriquet that reformer Walter Weyl in 1921 used to describe the spent Progressives of his age: "tired radicals." Indeed, they have become the great tenders of the nineties' culture wars, devoting incalculably more attention to

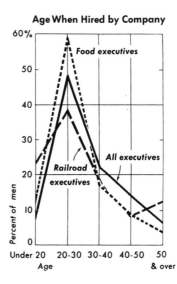

Age When Hired by Company

the symbolic defense of the National Endowment for the Arts than they have to the defense of the great shrinking welfare state. Curricular requirements at elite universities, or the tediously rehashed legacies of the sixties New Left campus revolt, invite more sustained comment among the left intelligentsia than wage inequality, strikes, or the explosion of the global sweatshop. As often as not, in fact, the global market's rhetoric of shopping-as-liberation is indistinguishable from our atrophied Left's allegiance to Lifestylismus—which is how an enterprise like *Wired* can simultaneously shill for global capitalism and brandish a nominally alternative, even revolutionary, edge.

Indeed, much of altcult politics nowadays has fallen, like the aesthetic and literary revolts of the twenties, into a facile, reflexive market libertarianism, which revolves around the classic libertarian aim of securing the optimal conditions of faux-daring self-expression. In the nineties Culture Bubble, this unfortunately reduces to the curious exercise of counterposing "new" media literacy and corporate brand allegiance to the straw demonology of cultural censorship. Today's cyber rebels trumpet their heroic exploits against the Helmses and Bennetts of our age, much as the bohemians of the twenties fancied themselves a fearless insurgency, scandalizing a nation of Comstocks and Protestant bluenoses with their ethos of literary realism and sexual liberation.

Even more unfortunately, *Wired* again provides the paradigmatic example of revolutionary cyber-

praxis, via the labors of its in-house prophet of political culture, Jon Katz. A former CBS news producer and NYU journalism school professor, Katz plies a vision of the republic eerily well-suited to the twenties campaign of self-styled literary radicals against a largely mythical Puritan culture. "Culture *is* politics" to today's young cyber-insurgents, Katz announces in his Digital Age manifesto, *Virtuous Reality*, which bears the fearless, incendiary subtitle, "How America Surrendered Discussion of Moral Values to Opportunists, Nitwits and Blockheads Like William Bennett."

Katz's estimation of the digital era's numberless virtues is every bit as nuanced and complicated as his reading of the culture wars. Tirelessly apostrophizing the "revolutionary," "free" and "democratic" virtues of the digital age, Katz detects samizdat rebellion bursting out of every e-mail account—he even, with embarrassing attention to detail, succumbs to a prolonged reverie of Revolutionary pamphleteer Tom Paine as a Web surfer. But since all the great Web controversies seem to take place within the terms of the Culture Bubble, the exercise of telling rude and liberating truths to power seems to concern matters a tad less world-historic than the questions that preoccupied Tom Paine. "The young have a moral right of access to the machinery and content of media and culture," Katz thunders, as though the central target demographic of the entire culture industry had been banished overnight by William Bennett into internment camps littered with books and broken radios. "Kids should not have to battle for the right to watch MTV," Katz goes on to declare, with admirable precision. Only in the giddy precincts of the Culture Bubble could the most banal of consumer choices—the freedom to watch frenetically edited advertisements—be worked up into a constitutive political "right." Nearly as laughable,

if they weren't so poignantly empty, are the shibboleths that, for Katz, comprise the "powerful sense of moral purpose" that, uh, "powers" digital culture: "Information wants to be free, individuals have the right to express themselves." Gee, that *is* revolutionary.

Whether it's Katz's hectoring, or the Ayn Rand-ish literary stylings of "Silicon Valley" novelist Po Bronson, or the countless cinematic, sitcom and indie rock productions that baptize gadget-happy entrepreneurs as latter-day Dantons, the Culture Bubble has quietly spread its gossamer casement around every conceivable outpost of would-be rebellion. In point of fact, of course, the matrix of prosperity in our own speculative times is nearly identical to the brutish global repression that William Allen White denounced with, to our ears, quaint moral outrage: Capital treads nimbly across more and more of the globe, romancing and discarding ever cheaper labor

markets and in the process consigning even the once comfortable middle class to downward wage pressure and chronic job insecurity. It took a global economic cataclysm for reformers like White to regain their voice in the wake of the twenties Culture Bubble; every one of the great questions that had recently exercised public opinion, from the revolt against literary gentility to the Prohibition crusade suddenly became embarrassingly puerile.

It's unlikely, of course, that a class-minded cease-fire is in the cards in our fin-de-siècle culture wars. So it probably behooves us to consider another, harsher verdict that the forward march of history levied upon another of the age's famed political unfortunates. Lincoln Steffens has won no small amount of infamy for pronouncing his wildly sanguine appraisal of the Soviet Union in the thirties: "I have seen the future, and it works." It has been far less eagerly recorded that in 1928 he, too, was a Hoover man. 🖎

Clistheret

I heard a sleave of song
  from an upper window
and moved in the sun to find them
I wanted to call to them,
  beg them to lean out,
and go on

But there was no window,
  I was on sand,
their lullabye came from the waves,
there were no waves,
  but a glinting derelict named—no derelict named
Delirious Iris, I am home, there is snow

from a filmy coal-blue sky, mechanical
  hissing, great heat, green clouds in the bath—please,
An eye in the lives of my loves
A lung in the lives of my loves
  and the two things You keep . . . keys:
to liberty, to manacle

           —Jeff Clark

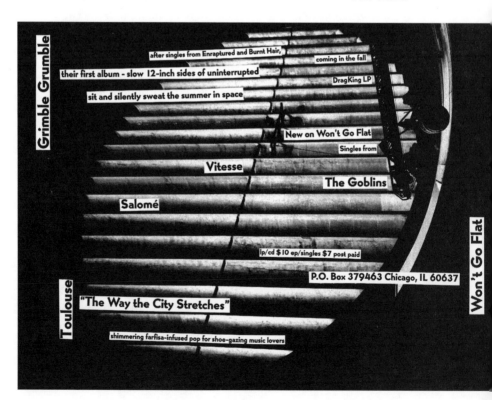

Pills

Your Personal Pamphlet

VIKI DILLON

1. How can I get some pills?

Getting pills is a breeze. Just select a psychiatrist from the Yellow Pages—and make an appointment! Mental health professionals will hand over a prescription without any fuss or bother. They like pills as much as you do!

Have you, at any point in your life, ever been a drug addict? Well, you might not want to mention that to your doctor. It may cause you both unnecessary worry—and who needs that? You don't *want* to worry. That's why you're taking the pills in the first place, right?

If something unpleasant about your past does slip out— *don't sweat it*. Most mental health professionals will overlook little things. . . such as your history of substance abuse. After all, prescription pills aren't illegal drugs, like the ones you took in college. They're the real thing: *medication*.

2. I read somewhere that pills are prescribed more often to women than to men. Should I let that disturb me?

Some people say it's easier for women to get pills from their doctors. Some people say this is bad. But the truth is, women need pills today. I know I do, and I'm a woman. You probably need them, too.

3. By the way, why should I take pills?

Cool people are taking pills. Hollywood actors. Supermodels. Artists on the cutting edge. Wild, up-and-coming rock stars. Pale people who wear black are taking them . . . and becoming vibrant and upbeat. Buttoned-down corporate drones are popping them . . . and relaxing. Pills are the ultimate fashion accessory: They're even making winners out of losers. But, hey, no pressure. The choice is up to you!

4. When do I need to take them?

You're not the type who reads instructions or follows

orders, are you? You're creative. And reckless. And impulsive. *You* decide.

Stuck? Can't think of a thing? Here are just a few ideas, to get you started:

9:00 a.m. Monday.

Right before that PRIVATE MEETING with your BOSS, a seventy-year-old alcoholic who runs one of the country's top pharmaceutical companies. Lately, he's been beefing up the advertising department . . . and that means he's paying lots of attention to YOU. The company's losing money fast! He needs to find markets for unnecessary products! You're under pressure! You've got to radiate self-confidence and sang-froid!

Skip the watery coffee and take a pill instead. This time, when he winks and slips you his home phone number, you won't miss a beat! Who has time to go through the legal department's six-volume report on sexual harassment? Just keep your wits about you. Treat him to some HOT IDEAS . . . about product development and innovative marketing. Keep smiling! Brush his hand off your thigh and show him your passion is for BUSINESS.

11:25 a.m. Monday.

You run into an ATTRACTIVE, MARRIED CO-WORKER at the water cooler. So what if he never called you back after you FOOLED AROUND TOGETHER in the darkened mailroom during the office CHRISTMAS PARTY. So what if it'll soon be against company policy for staff members to DATE. If it suits your style, ignore the rules. Who can keep up with them, anyway? Be coy, charming . . . *and* aggressive. Ask him out to lunch.

1:10 p.m. Monday.

Almost time for that LUNCH DATE. Don't get NERVOUS and blow it! Take a pill, instead. Stay poised! Be friendly, open, and available. Act aloof. Play hard to get.

Feel like you're juggling a bunch of awkward, contradictory FEMININE ROLES? Are you cast as a powerful AMAZON in the morning, a BITCH in the afternoon, and a HELPLESS VICTIM the next day? Don't even try to figure it out. You've come a long way, baby. Hang in there! Pop an extra one! Just be yourself.

3:11 p.m. Monday.

You've just designed a witty, tongue-in-cheek brochure about PILLS. It's a work of advertising genius. But your older, more experienced, and better-paid COMPETITOR takes credit for it—just like he did the last time, and the time before that. Don't get so ANGRY that you start to shake all over! Get revenge.

Why not change the copy on the brochure, ever so slightly? Now, something is SERIOUSLY ASKEW. Send it off to the printer, and send a hundred thousand copies through the mail. Distribute your PERSONAL PAMPHLET to the WORLD!

6:40 p.m. Monday.

Just this once, you manage to sneak out of the office before nine o'clock at night—two hours early. But, thanks to your unexpected change in schedule, you run into your old GIRLFRIEND on the street. Why let unresolved RELATIONSHIPS or conflicts about your SEXUALITY get you down? Take a pill! Join her for an early dinner! (And try to share your feelings about your pills. Remember: Your friend might like to have some of her own!)

9:00 p.m. Monday.

You stop at the all-night supermarket and bring a bag of groceries to your aging, sickly, housebound FATHER who REPEATEDLY MOLESTED you when you were a child! There's no reason to hold grudges, is there? And what have you got to be afraid of? You're invulnerable, as long as you've got those pills! Don't forget . . . he's slowly dying of CANCER! He's got one year to live. Uh, oh. Time to overcome your AMBIVALENCE and tell him that you LOVE him before it's TOO LATE. And even though death and ILLNESS are REAL BAD NEWS, you can handle them. You've done it before, haven't you? If you live in New York or Chicago or L.A . . . . *any* place, really . . . at least one of your friends have already DIED of AIDS by now. No need to get unhinged, though. Confront mortality—WITHOUT PAIN!

10:10 p.m. Monday.

You take the SUBWAY to your apartment. Worried about that guy carrying a GUN? Or the lunatic who's exposing his GENITALS to you? Relax. You can deal. It happens every day, right? You know what to do.

11:30 p.m. Monday.

Your ATTRACTIVE, MARRIED COLLEAGUE shows up unexpectedly, right on your doorstep! He's feeling AMOROUS. Don't be ill at ease! Invite him upstairs. Or, tell him to get lost. Make the first move. Or, take a CLASSIC strategy and BE REAL PASSIVE . . . just WAIT AND SEE what *he* does! Anyway, why be hung up about it? It's all the same to you! You're on medication! And, when things get down to brass tacks, you'll handle that sticky conversation about AIDS and SAFE SEX—no problem!

9:00 a.m. Tuesday.

Your attractive colleague turned out to have a VIOLENT streak. Luckily, you're SUPER HIP, and you know how to PLAY IT ROUGH. You don't mind a little PHYSICAL BRUTALITY or SADISM now and then! Just cover those BRUISES with the perfect foundation to match your skin tone! Put your pills in your pocket and head out for that SUBWAY. Another shooting on the subway platform? Ambulance and police cars gonna make you late for work? Go on, admit it. You don't give a shit! It's a brand new day! You're sedated—heavily—and, girl, you're READY FOR ANYTHING that comes!

This brochure courtesy of the Munroe Drug Company.

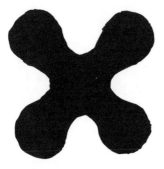 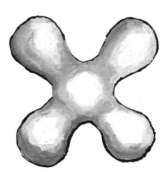

You're Either On the Bus . . .

Kim Phillips-Fein

EVERY morning at 5:30 a.m. the buses roll into the ghetto. They stop to pick up their cargo of dark-skinned workers, then turn around and drive out to the region just beyond the city limits— the place where anyone can find work. Once in the industrial districts of the suburbs, the bus makes several stops, letting workers off at electronics factories, warehouses, and the like. At night the workers climb back onto the buses and are taken away to the depths of the city once again.

Johannesburg in 1988? No, Chicago in 1997. The bus company isn't some cog of South Africa's apartheid machine—it's the feel-good, ultra-responsible Bridges-to-Work program, the latest pet project of the John D. and Catherine T. MacArthur Foundation. Bridges-to-Work typifies what passes for social policy in America these days, as foundations, charities, and corporations step in to fill the gulf left by Big Government. After all, even liberals have bought into a hard-headed post-Reagan "realism." Social spending is no more than stingy charity writ large; there's not much public spending can do to change the morals of the underclass. We've got to provide make-work jobs to teach them a work ethic, Big Brothers to offer positive role models, group therapy sessions to inculcate self-esteem. And we've got to offer up the poor as the perfect workers—desperate, weak, non-union, and malleable—for their own good, as well as ours. Ready for the ride?

Bridges-to-Work, currently in pilot stage in five cities, is set up to perform two main functions: to place inner-city job seekers in entry-level, blue-collar positions in suburbia, and to provide cheap transportation to get them there. The program, which is nonprofit, promises to be everything that the welfare state isn't: It's relatively cheap (the pilot programs will cost $17 million over the next two years), benefits the rich and the poor at the same time and it hands nobody a free lunch. Its historical faiths are as simple as its solutions: Everything was fine in urban America until the early 1970s, when technological innovation and global competition drove businesses out of the city, forcing all the brave new factories to open their doors on the cheap land of the suburban frontier. Hence "pockets of poverty" and bastions of unemployment were created in the inner city, innumerable social pathologies following inevitably in their wake.

See Me, Feel Me, Touch Me, Accumulate Me

Thomas Goetz

Despite five years of solid economic growth, ten years of impressive corporate profits, and fifteen years of a stock market so bullish that finance pundits are talking of a "new paradigm," some Americans still worry about money. No, not those petty worries about not having money—how will we pay the rent, where will the food come to feed our children, and so forth—but rather those concerns that come with having it, and wanting to make more of it.

For those who fret over where to put their money, or how to invest it, or simply how to enjoy possessing it, there is a new breed of book ready to alleviate our fears and let us invest with impunity: Call it self-actualized investment. Like baseball players praising God for their talent and $30 million-five-year contract, America's investors are turning to self-actualized investment guides to feel at ease with the dumb luck the stock market has showered on them. Within the last year, as the stock market has continued to reach record heights, the new field of self-actualized investment books has blossomed with it. There's already been one bestseller—Suze Ormand's **Nine Steps to Financial Freedom.** A slew of hopefuls, all promising you the same rosy disposition, is on the way.

Self-actualized investment combines

Where once there were jobs, hardworking men and cheery housewives, now there is only gang rule, teen parenthood and bombed-out buildings. To urban planners, blinkered by their focus on the urban labor market, the culture of joblessness and the blight that accompanies it appear intractable—the city hemorrhages jobs, the ghetto expands, while city pols look on helplessly.

But not so the brave visionaries at Bridges-to-Work. The problem with architects of the conventional "antipoverty" strategies, says Mark Allen Hughes, the Kennedy School grad behind the Bridges-to-Work dream, is that they're too fixated on the city limits. Urban planners must redraw their "mental maps" to reflect changes in "metropolitan settlement structure"—i.e., white flight and the shuttering of large Chicago factories like International Harvester and U.S. Steel. Poverty isn't just an economic question, it's an exercise in geography. As Hughes wrote in *Over the Horizon*, a 1993 report funded by the Ford Foundation, "Most antipoverty strategies are attempts to change geography." Hughes notes the obvious: Disparities of wealth and poverty, employment and unemployment, manifest themselves geographically. Inner-city neighborhoods are rife with social pathologies and idle adults, while in the pristine landscapes of suburbia, employers "search the suburbs for workers to fill the entry level jobs which dominate the labor market." But with a little creative cartography, Hughes suggests, policymakers can do an end-run around geographical realities: Simply "connect the dots." Take the people to the jobs, and urban unemployment (and hence poverty) will vanish—welfare mothers will achieve self-sufficiency, indigent fathers will start making child-support payments, and young people might even sign up for a bus ride instead of joining a gang.

The Bridges-to-Work imagery is one of doors, thresholds, frontiers. "Jobs are no longer around the corner," Hughes maintains. "Jobs are over the horizon." You may have thought your options were limited—but all the while there was a whole new world just out of eyesight, a "geography of opportunity" full of employers and workers running toward each other in slow motion while the theme from *Chariots of Fire* surged in the background. Bridges-to-Work will "stabilize" inner-city neighborhoods so that black residents won't have to move to the suburbs to find jobs. And the millions of dollars in wages brought back to the city by newly employed residents will cause a thousand retail stores to blossom and a thousand multiplier effects to bloom. "It's a win-win-win situation," chimes a Bridges-to-Work promotional brochure—for the worker, for the employer, for the suburbanite who gets to keep his picket fence lily-white.

Bridges-to-Work is one of several job-counseling programs Hughes operates through a non-profit organization, Public/Private Ventures. The outfit's board of directors is packed with luminaries ranging from liberal academic William Julius Wilson to conservative criminologist (and rhetorical superpredator) John DiIulio. It's a charming bipartisan effort: Wilson advocates Bridges-to-Work-style programs—at least as a "short-term solution"—in his 1996 book, *When Work Disappears*, and has said elsewhere that reverse-commuting programs represent "the most important antipoverty research and development initiative of our time." DiIulio, on the other hand, has argued that conventional welfare programs have bred a generation of monsters in the inner cities. At the urging of the Ford Foundation, Public/Private Ventures set up Bridges-to-Work programs in Baltimore, Philadelphia, Denver, St. Louis, Minneapolis and Chicago in 1996, receiving funding from the Department of Housing and Urban Development, Ford, MacArthur, the Pew Charitable Trust, and a host of local governments. If these pilot programs go well, the Clinton administration has promised to O.K. funding for forty new demonstration sites in the year 2000.

When most dreamy new social programs intended to aid the urban poor are introduced—remember midnight basketball?—there's little to do but wait for the program to fail, and then submit to another round of hand-wringing about how ineffective federal programs are in alleviating urban poverty. But in the case of Bridges-to-Work, we actually have an existing example of the program to hold up as a model: the Chicago chapter, Suburban JobLink, has been busing the poor to the suburbs since the early eighties. Founded as an employment agency in the early seventies by Catholic activist John Plunkett, Suburban JobLink has won the plaudits of Chicago newspapers as varied as the *Defender*, the legendary black daily, and the politically orthodox *Tribune*. And why shouldn't the city's opinion-makers love it? It's a "politically feasible" way to deal with the urban poor, right?

the put-yourself-first appeal of Tony Robbins with the spreadsheet acumen of financial authors like Jane Bryant Quinn or Peter Lynch. The animating idea might be described as feeling good about feeling greedy. The timing couldn't be better. In the nineties, the level of participation in the stock market by so-called non-institutional investors has reached unprecedented levels. Common citizens with more-than-common wealth have eschewed traditional caches such as bank accounts and treasury bonds in favor of the no-frills world of no-load mutual funds. They've even chucked their brokers, trusting instead in the relatively cheap advice of tipsheets like **Smartmoney**.

The democratizing wonders of the Invisible Hand, right? Maybe. Another way to look at it is that these do-it-yourself pikers are driving the market to dangerously narcotic highs. It's as if the top quarter of the U.S. income bracket went in on a trillion-dollar Ponzi scheme—but unlike Albania, everyone has somehow come out on top. Maybe it will last, maybe it won't. But in the meantime, mere riches have done little to assuage the anxiety—and guilt—that comes with being in on the most craven financial rapine in half a century.

Which is where Suze Ormand comes in. Noting the distress that has come with success, Ormand has crafted nine "Practical and Spiritual Steps so You Can Stop Worrying," a three-tiered strategy for readers to reach financial freedom—that mythic state where our money works for us, our affairs are in order, and financial advisers (like Ormand) are unnecessary. But if we're to achieve that heightened state, we'd better know what we're dealing with. "Money is a living entity," she writes. "It is drawn to those who welcome it, those who respect it. Wouldn't you rather be with people who respect you and who don't want you to be something you're not? Your money feels the same way."

Despite her wacky anthropo-morphizing and new-age tone, Ormand's finance credentials aren't easy to dismiss. Trained at Merrill Lynch, she did a stint as vice-president of investments at Prudential-Bache. So when she writes stuff like "one way to get in touch with your money is to actually start touching it again," she deserves to be taken seriously—or at least as seriously as anybody else who purports to dispense financial advice. Certainly the book-buying public agrees: Her book was perched on bestseller lists for months after its release last spring.

If Ormand has inaugurated a new self-help genre, it's because she stood on the shoulders of giants—or Deepak Chopra, anyway. Since the early eighties, Chopra has preached a distinctly worldly spiritualism, where focus, centering, and other vague notions can lead to great emotional and financial success. Millions of readers bought it, as Chopra's puffball materialism turned into a multi-volume, million-dollar empire. More recently, Stephen Covey has spun his Mormon faith into one of the decade's biggest sellers, **The Seven Habits of Highly Effective People**, a common-sense checklist by which readers might organize their daily lives in a strict, distinctly corporate framework.

So it comes as little surprise that with business and finance now seeping into every slot of life from weekend movie grosses to the burger wars, self-help and finance might miscegenate into a new genre. "If you read ordinary financial books, they tell you how you must get your priorities in order," notes Peter Ginna, who edited Ormand's book at Crown and now works at Oxford University Press. "But that's almost the province of therapy for some people. You first have to get people to the place where they can make those practical

Who could possibly object to the idea? Suburbanites, corporations, transit mavens, inner-city youth—it's a coalition to end all coalitions, a consensus-builder's dream. It won't cost anyone a dime.

If the experience of Suburban JobLink is any indication, however, Bridges-to-Work won't amount to much more than an easy cop-out for the "socially conscious," and a low-wage labor windfall for suburban employers. The real promise of Bridges-to-Work, as a close scrutiny of the Chicago experiment reveals, is nothing other than the allure of the temp economy, tricked out in the pious language of foundation liberalism rather than the simply exploitative language of "flexibility" and zero benefits.

Before beginning its busing service, Suburban JobLink opened in the early seventies as a non-profit contracting service. It paid higher wages than the other industrial temp services, and eventually became popular among workers, winning accounts away from other contracting services. During the eighties, Suburban JobLink lowered its wage rates, going down to minimum wage on new accounts, supposedly in order to shift resources toward finding full-time jobs for workers.

It's not difficult to see how such a move would substantially improve the bottom line of its operating budget. In 1995, the group received $625,000 in public and foundation funds but brought in more than $5 million in revenues from temp contracting. The organization claims a much smaller markup on each temp than corporate agencies do, so workers see more of the agency fee in their wages. But what Suburban JobLink is doing—bargaining down the average wage for entry-level jobs—is fundamentally not too different from what Manpower and Ready-Men have done for years in poor Chicago neighborhoods. The only difference is that Manpower (which is currently going after welfare mothers with a vengeance) isn't applauded for offering a new social vision.

Of course, if Suburban JobLink was able to place large numbers of poor Chicagoans in full-time jobs, even doubters would have to deem the program a success (though you'd still have to ask if the city of Chicago should really be subsidizing the transportation of workers to suburban factories). But Suburban JobLink has been remarkably unsuccessful at placing its workers in full-time suburban employment. According to the Mayor's Office of Employment and Training, Suburban JobLink was able to place only about 435 workers in full-time suburban jobs in 1996. With numbers like this, the goals of the organization can't be too ambitious; Plunkett's dream, which he admits he's never been able to achieve, is to place 1,000 people a year in full-time suburban jobs. Meanwhile, Chicago has an unemployed population of 77,000. (Economic growth in the city has created more than 12,000 jobs since 1993—far more than Suburban JobLink could possibly bus to the burbs.) What's more, many of the people on Suburban JobLink buses aren't full-time workers at all—according to its most recent financial reports, some 400 temp workers still ride the buses each day. So Suburban JobLink is still at least as much a temp agency as an employment service—a fact mentioned nowhere in the MacArthur Foundation's glowing reports, let alone the laudatory editorials in the *Tribune* and *Defender*.

Naturally, the fact that the latest solution to entrenched poverty is actually little more than a glorified temp agency is not something its inventors wish to publicize. Suburban JobLink officials are oddly reticent about the exact proportion of temp workers to full-time workers on their buses. "We just don't have those numbers, and I wouldn't want to guess on something like this," says David Boyd, the organization's director of community outreach.

And, as I discovered when I visited the organization's offices, Suburban JobLink sure acts more like a temp service than a full-time employment agency. When I showed up and said I was looking for work, the woman behind the desk told me there were no openings at the moment. She then handed me a list of other temporary agencies I should contact, including Ready-Men and Manpower. I told her I wanted one of the full-time jobs; she told me that Suburban JobLink only took people as the agency needed them, and that all the jobs offered by Suburban JobLink were minimum-wage anyway. "Try another agency," she suggested. Next to me, a woman registered with the agency asked if there was any work; she was told to come by the next morning, as work groups for the day were assigned—clearly a temporary assignment.

One could overlook these flaws if Suburban JobLink actually managed to provide some kind of relief to the

decisions."

Not that much of the welter of self-actualized investment advice now coming onto the market is of much practical use. To her credit, Ormand pauses now and then from her Jungnastics to explain the particulars of 401(k) plans and fixed-versus-variable rate mortgages. Not so some other hacks now scurrying to cash in on the new genre. In **Don't Worry, Make Money**, for instance, Richard Carlson traces his investment strategy to a Wall Street guru named Bobby McFerrin: "When Bobby McFerrin first sang his classic song, 'Don't Worry, Be Happy,' I felt as if he were singing my thoughts to the world," Carlson writes. "I began to realize that the same essential idea applies to success and money." From there, it's on to Kenny Rogers' "know when to hold 'em, know when to fold 'em" (or as Carlson garbles it, "know when to bet, when to hold, and when to fold"), and the Seven Dwarves' "whistle while you work." Not exactly advice worth paying for but, then, Carlson's previous, no less witless book, **Don't Sweat the Small Stuff**, tops the **New York Times** bestseller list as of this writing.

Which makes his brand of therapy all the more unsettling. "Worry keeps us from feeling free and joyful. We are never truly free until we break the chains of fear," Carlson writes. "Developing wealth consciousness is what this book is all about. Wealth consciousness suggests a complete absence of money worries; an awareness that there is always plenty of money to go around." Besides the fact that Carlson's "plenty to go around" claim is an affront to the majority of Americans, these assurances hardly apply even for the most comfortable reader in Carlson's upper-middle-class target audience. But it isn't Carlson's task to reiterate the plain fact of American income disparity, or even to explain away bourgeois guilt about such facts. He's writing to exorcise such concerns from his readers psychic portfolios. Carlson has one simple goal: to leave readers with the impression that they deserve every penny they possess, and that they should feel no compunction about exploiting every asset to make more.

"Everybody approaches money and investing with a highly charged emotional state," says John Schott, author of the forthcoming **Mind Over Money: How to Match Your Emotional Style to a Winning Financial Strategy**. "Some people let their greed get out of hand, while others show this moral masochism by holding onto bad stocks as if to punish themselves. Psychological investing involves mastering these emotions."

More than Ormand or Carlson, Schott—a practicing psychiatrist on the Harvard Medical School faculty, as well as an investment manager with a $160 million portfolio—is forthright about who he's writing for. He provides seven or eight different personality types—"The Power Investor," say, or "The Thrill Seeker"—and shows how each temperament creates unnecessary risks. "As people read, they'll see some things of themselves," he explains.

Or perhaps they'll see just how inverted these authors' conceptions of reality are. While Ormand argues that a proper respect for their money is "one of the reasons the rich get richer," for instance, she handily skips over the main reason they get richer: capital's tendency to accumulate (and capitalists' tendency to ensure social conditions under which their interests are protected). Perhaps it's **other people's** respect for their money that makes the rich so happy and worry-free.

Those kinds of thoughts, of course, have to be kept safely behind a shroud of Blavatskian charlatanry. Ormand, for instance, leads her readers through a

chronically unemployed, most of whom live in the large swathes of the city where a majority of the residents are unemployed for long periods of time—notably in the large housing projects and in many South and West Side neighborhoods. But Suburban JobLink actually doesn't target neighborhoods with the lowest labor-force participation rate—its bus route runs by only one of the housing projects, and there's no reason to believe recruitment from the project is particularly high, especially since, once again, the organization claimed no relevant statistics were available. In reality, most people who find employment through Suburban JobLink are people who could probably have found work through any temp agency or through their own initiative. Like the other Bridges-to-Work projects it has an elaborate screening process for applicants to make sure that they are "work-ready": literate, properly deferential, and available for work immediately.

But the reasons for inner-city unemployment run much deeper than a lack of transportation. The notorious Cabrini-Green housing project, for example, borders tony, service-job-rich Lincoln Park; the same is the case for the seriously depressed Oakland and Woodlawn neighborhoods, both of which are a stone's throw from the University of Chicago and its massive hospitals. Inadequate education, lack of child care, and the unwillingness of employers to hire young black men for even the most menial of jobs have as much effect on people in these neighborhoods as just not having a ride. Even Plunkett admits that many suburban employers don't want to hire black workers; they frequently request Mexican temps and refuse to hire African-Americans. In the long run, this would seem to present serious problems with the Suburban JobLink strategy. Plunkett, to his credit, won't do business with such employers. But he is also reluctant to identify those companies publicly because "if we were to become visibly identified as rabble rousers, we'd be out of business," he says. "That tag would just blow us out of the industry."

Of course, if unemployment were the sole cause of urban poverty, then turning cities into bedroom communities for a mobile low-wage labor force might just solve all these problems. But it's just not so. Yes, it's true that most extremely poor neighborhoods in the city have unemployment rates of 15 percent or higher. But even in these neighborhoods poverty rates tend to be higher than unemployment rates—which isn't surprising when you remember that there are nearly 49,000 working families in Chicago living below the poverty line. Lousy jobs, not just long-term unemployment, account for much of the misery in Chicago's poor neighborhoods.

Take South Austin, one of the West Side neighborhoods Suburban JobLink draws on heavily. By anybody's standards, it's a pretty poor place. Median income is $14,500 a year, and a high proportion of the neighborhood's families receive public assistance. Among the working population (the labor force participation rate of 57 percent is slightly lower than that for the city as a whole) unemployment runs about 20 percent. This is high, of course; it's about what the national unemployment rate was during the Depression. Even so, it doesn't lend itself to William Julius Wilson's evocations of neighborhoods from which the daily rhythms of work have disappeared entirely. The working poor of a neighborhood like South Austin aren't poor because of some cultural deficiency or other, let alone as a result of geography— they're poor because they work in jobs that don't pay enough. For them, as for most poor people, poverty isn't a question of total separation from the labor market; it's a definite kind of participation in working life, cycling through short-term jobs that are dull, physically difficult, and poorly paid.

These sorts of considerations don't seem to matter to the Bridges-to-Work ideologues. For them (as for their colleagues at the foundations or in New Democratic circles), whether or not you're employed is a question of character, of moral worth, of good culture; in a sense, the nature of the job is irrelevant—all that matters is that you're working. The "new urban poor" are amoral, self-defeating gangbangers and welfare queens because they have become unhinged from work, and hence from familial responsibility. As Wilson wrote in *When Work Disappears*, "A neighborhood in which people are poor but employed is different from a neighborhood in which people are poor and jobless . . . . Work is not simply a way to make a living and support one's family. It also constitutes a framework for daily behavior, because it imposes discipline.... In the absence of regular employment, life, including family life, becomes less coherent." In a recent *Washington Post* article about a program that trains wel-

sort of repressed memory session: "Think back and see that your feelings about money today . . . can almost certainly be traced to an incident, possibly forgotten until now, from your past," she writes. This state of suspended emotion—where we disinter our money worries in order to bury them again—is manifest throughout the genre.

But for all their Panglossian gloss, these authors and their publishers know that they're exposed to as much risk as, say, any Wall Street jockey going "Texas long" in the options markets. A stock market correction or two or three bearish years, could stick them with lots of unsold books. With two years of writing behind him and several months yet to go before his January publication date, Schott even admits to being anxious about it. "I've been hoping nothing bad happens," he says. "I want the book to come out now." Whether or not self-actualized investment can endure if the market turns sour—or if it may be, like the return of the three piece suit and the celebrity of Jakob Dylan, just another symptom of irrational exuberance—is yet to be seen. But until the bears are back in force, the book business is exulting in its latest creation. "Publishing being what it is," Ginna rightly notes, "with a couple bestsellers like this, there'll be dozens more on the way."

fare recipients to clean toilets for a living, Katherine Boo captured today's sensibilities perfectly: "Grow up, get real, get a job—any job at all." Suburban JobLink, like many liberal organizations, equates any job with a good job—which is sensible only if the primary purpose of work is its moral utility, if installing a work ethic is at least as important as pulling a salary that can support your family.

This happens to be a pretty convenient hypothesis, since jobs in Edge City, on average, pay less than those in the city, and sometimes the pay is much worse. Average weekly manufacturing wages are $789 in Cook County (where Chicago is) compared to $635 in Lake County (immediately north of the city); weekly retail wages are $317 a week in Cook, and $267 in Lake. (The difference is somewhat less stark for DuPage County; retail wages are actually higher than those in Cook. Of course, it's more than a half-hour's drive from the ghetto.) Chicago suburbs may be job-rich but they are wage-poor. Unions tell horror stories of city-suburb wage differentials; one company, Kimco, paid its city janitors $11.05 an hour plus full benefits, while janitors at its suburban outposts earned $5.50 an hour with no benefits. Almost none of the companies Suburban JobLink works with are unionized. Maybe Bridges-to-Work is right to emphasize the "stabilizing" qualities of the program; its workers certainly won't be buying houses in the far burbs of Lake County anytime soon.

But even though Suburban JobLink is little more than a sham now doesn't mean that a similar program couldn't work in the future. Af-

ter all, with John DiIulio's support, anything can happen—one morning great fleets of gleaming buses may be rolling down Chicago's grimy streets, driving lots of full-time workers out to jobs in the burbs. But even on such a massive scale—say they built a foundation-run subway system—the idea still won't work. First of all, public transit schemes just don't make sense in the low-density burbs: there's no central point from which jobs are easily accessible. Instead, special lines would have to take workers to each individual workplace, a project which local governments might find overwhelming even in times when public transit was in better shape. Second, transporting all those grateful city-dwellers to the suburbs won't affect the fundamental forces that have led to central-city decline and the dispersal of population and jobs. Inner-ring suburbs suffer from the same economic ailments as the central city, and the suburban areas with the most rapidly expanding employment tend to be those the farthest away from the city.

This raises one of the central contradictions with which "mobility" programs are designed to grapple. Workers—like factories—are of a fundamentally different nature than capital, which can be transformed into money to be deployed and redeployed in any anonymous landscape, slipping easily to wherever it can get the highest return. But workers are rooted: They have homes and families in the city and can't so easily be moved. The geniuses behind Bridges-to-Work insist nonetheless on making workers as fluid and mobile as capital itself, busing them for hours to whatever far-off burb is experiencing this year's boom.

Yet at the same time, they imagine an essentially stagnant workforce. The key to the Bridges-to-Work myth is the assumption that once employed, inner-city residents will stay in the inner city, instead of joining their new bosses in the burbs. This is why it wouldn't serve the same function for the Chicago Transit Authority to run a few bus lines between Chicago and its suburbs: Because then poor people wouldn't just be bused from home to work, from work to home. They could use the libraries, the parks, the miniature golf courses. They could eat in suburban restaurants and shop in suburban malls and go to the suburban supermarkets on the way home from work. So when Suburban JobLink negotiates with Pace (metro Chicago's public bus system) to extend its services, it does not argue simply for expanded public transit between the city and its suburbs, but for Pace to replicate Suburban JobLink and take people straight to the factories where they work. In the past year, thanks to the efforts of Suburban JobLink, Pace has initiated two "Avon Express" lines to bus workers out to Avon production plants in suburban Morton Grove. Pace also leases vans to Suburban JobLink so that the organization can

more easily transport workers directly to their jobs. After all, creating genuine connections between the city and the suburbs would destroy suburbia's entire *raison d'être*.

It's easy to understand the appeal of programs like Suburban JobLink and Bridges-to-Work. Using the language of bridge-building, network-establishing, and connection-forming, the organizations put forward a solution to the problems of poverty that is expressed entirely in capital's terms. Never mind that the city is in trouble because of a massive shift of resources to suburbia and the rural hinterlands; never mind that lower wages for workers mean higher profits for the boss. And especially forget that real, permanent solutions to urban poverty will require a redistribution of wealth—and that means some sort of fight. Conflict is something the foundation liberals want no part of, preferring instead to indulge an endless succession of philanthropic programs designed to treat the sufferers in our midst, to console them, analyze them, bind their wounds, and offer them up as subjects for any experiment a social scientist can dream up. If you're a Ph.D. with a great new solution for the urban crisis involving nothing more than nice things like basketballs, parks, or bus rides, we're sure the poor will be happy to oblige.

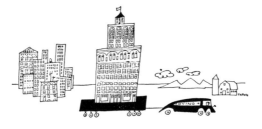

Cordon Sanitaire

SETH SANDERS

Amps for Christ: *The Secret of the Almost Straight Line* 7" ep (Westside Audio Laboratories)

Barnes was the man behind Man is the Bastard's gruesome and gigantic howl (they almost made me give up meat; no, I'm MORE cynical than you are). Here the pain comes back as love. These shimmering musical fragments ("Pure Hammond"; "1-2 Stomp") are angels' harps, built from junkyard skeletons, in action; the opposite of trance music.

Atari Teenage Riot: *Burn, Berlin, Burn!* cd (Grand Royal)

Just one of the dizzying, delicious things about this record is how uncool it is. That is to say that it's over the top, unfocused, viciously self-righteous, pounding, insistent, and annoying, which is everything that our knowing, ironic pop culture and its bullshit self-confidence would rather look away from. It's as if all the Generation X ambivalence came back as disturbingly unfocused rage—pounding hateful generic thrash that we're all supposed to have listened to in "the eighties" (I think you were in a room with Thomas Dolby at the time)—and as if its eagerness for hip new products came back as a desire to chew paint off walls; ATR's closeness to Oi (the massive ripoff of Sham 69[they were an oi band]'s "If the Kids Are United"; the chanting and shouting), Death (the massive ripoff of Slayer[they are a Death Metal band]'s "Angel of Death" [it was about Mengele; he was a Nazi doctor; do you remember the Nazis? They were the villains

in *Schindler's List*], recast as a scheme of classification on "Into the Death" [a simple list: 1) fight! 2) war! 3) fire! 4) violence! 5) death! 6) TV! 7) police! 8) FUCK YOU!!!!!!!!!!]), punk rock ("Sick to Death" loops not one but *two* Users [they were 12-foot-tall dancing gay street urchins] riffs, "Sick of You" and "Decadent Jew," into a giddy realization: Revulsion and disgust are sources of power), hardcore (who cares if "Fuck All" is peeled, stem to stern, from the Bad Brains' [potsmoking Rasta jazz musicians who whipped the little white kids' asses at playing fast and loud] "Pay to Cum"; after all, they were just stealing the little white kids' culture!), Techno (whatever), all combine to make them a little too preachy (though nobody was quite sure what they were preaching and they used the phrase well, anyway in the middle of their supposed political platforms, as if their ideas were forming at the same time as the music or that Godforfuckingbid they understood irony and confusion as well as you do) and insistent (they probably hate you) for your average, gentle Tortoise [a great murky studio production outfit with a lot of silly fans, much like Sean Puffy Combs] fan. Most embarassing of all, this music's incredibly complicated and confusing, and they mean all of it and they're right. Record of the motherfucking century.

Behead the Prophet No Lord Shall Live: *I Am That Great and Fiery Force* CD/LP (K/Outpunk)

Songs about a lover who'll only make

love when you're sleeping (is he a crypto-necro or just scared?); Venom samples (the original Confused Black Metal band described by bassist Kronos, remorseful and pissed, as Satanism, fucking stupidity, and smokebombs going off everywhere, or something . . .); and an extended metaphor where a horny gay man is an obscene tank driver: This is hardcore gone one step further. The sound is indecipherable at first (yes, that's a violin) but the cluttered midrange, continually in violent motion, is really a closetful of horror movies, love letters, porno pictures, and shaky childish drawings, crammed beyond bursting and exploding into my face. As your head catches up (or slows down, Charles Bronson fans) to the pulse, you hear choruses, hoots, hollers, Lynyrd Skynyrd. . . . On the tenth listen to "All Day Interference" it's all clear: There was never any other way to say it.

Charles Bronson/Quill: split 7" ep (Nat, JAPAN)

While Charles Bronson are able to summon more self-righteous venom than your ex-wife digging her claws into your face, they've also got a wiseass, corrosive sense of humor (public-service announcements with orchestral accompaniment?) and even wiser aphorisms (Black Metal bands should print shirts with logos that people can actually fucking read; let's start a revolution so I can break some shit.); in between making fun of themselves they vomit out a seamless, ridiculously dynamic wall of battery that make Void, Siege and Venom [foam-at-the-mouthers who make people look like a bunch of candy-asses] look like a bunch of candy-asses; not a dead second. Too bad they split up. On the flip, Quill spew motorboat froth and an awesome Intense Degree cover. Yes, hardcore continues to go off years after you stopped listening to Minor Threat; yes, they actually mean it; now go ladle some more bored indie irony onto a fresh slice of electronica.

Los Crudos: *Canciones Para Liberar Nuestras Fronteras* lp (self-released)

Virtually all in Spanish, completely all at the top of their lungs, a big handful of thumbtacks. While I could do with more overt screeches or roars, or even more passages of rhythm and texture not overlaid by jitters and shouting, there's something bold and warm about this, like a trumpet. One of the few things to come out of Chicago (cf. Naked Raygun's singsong *Home of the Brave*) that makes me feel patriotic.

Jean Dubuffet: *Les Expériences Musicales du Jean Dubuffet* cd (Mandala, dist. by Harmona Mundi)

Jean Dubuffet was the founder of an aesthetic movement called "Art Brut" which took the works of children and the insane seriously as art. While interest in the Primitive is very easily reducible to a "white quest for authenticity," (raw, unrestrained, stupid people are closer to the vital pulse of the universe, in touch with the unconscious, and can reinvigorate our flagging Lounge Culture) the music on this cd is also reducible, in a move approximately as swift, to "just a bunch of ones and zeros." A number of Dubuffet's lunatics were, in fact, brilliant; among the works collected in his museum in Lausanne are monuments and miniatures, products of enormous effort and craftsmanship, and, yes, some pieces of searing intensity as well as crystalline beauty. Just as importantly, they were human, and caring about them lets us better understand the human thing. As far as the lunatics' art goes, it is the *systematized* quality of many of their works that remains with a visitor. What makes certain of the giant, decorated paintings so disturbing is the desire to extend, to balance and to justify the visual forms, the inability to leave something alone. In some way they are thus more like legal systems or religions than paintings; fear of, or contempt for, these is really a terror of the mind itself.

When I first heard this disc's lead-off track I was astonished by the sheer nerve; Dubuffet had multi-tracked his own voice chanting, for 23 minutes, about a beard of flowers. The French language's rich liquids and back vowels were never more fully realized than in his triumphal drone: "Le

FLEUR du BARBE!!" Upon reflection, perhaps this isn't as well-crafted as John Coltrane's *Africa/Brass*. Every minute does not count, and the details are not crucial. Reading Dubuffet's own comments, I understood that this was the point, and that it helped make it better, not worse, art. The songs on this disc, an alternate version of which had already appeared as a bootleg lp, are rumored to come from a six-lp box that was originally released in an edition of fifty. This is worth noting because of the negative reaction that Dubuffet seemed to anticipate in the notes. While such facts and such a history would normally make this merely a consolation prize in lieu of the original for avant-garde collectors, it is not they who need to hear it. It's more normal people to whom this might give pause, who could find something here for themselves, and revel in the power of their own voice and noise.

Missy Misdemeanor Elliott: *Supa Dupa Fly* cd (Elektra)

Almost alone among contemporary R&B artists, Missy Elliott does not take off her shirt. Or even wear shorts. What she does is wink, smile, sway slightly, polish her green leather overalls, and crack wise ("I'm suuuuuuuuch a good rapperrrr"). And she is. While only the designated A-bomb single and a few other tracks really lay down that dense web of lurching beats, surprising hooks, and loopy-ass jokes, when Missy fires on all cylinders they are cylinders from a spaceship equipped with a truly amazing selection of tropical drinks.

Gerty Farish/Pissed Officers: *Help Gerty Farish and the Pissed Officers Save the Ants* split 10" (not on a record label)

The time: "the eighties." The place: a jerry-built, highly flammable fake Gothic campus in the Hollywood English countryside, set for the filming of the biggest Thomas Dolby video EVER. In the background, some mawkish bleeps and bloops set the mood; everything is calm, if contrived, when suddenly—DISASTER: Thomas's hair has caught fire in the Bunsen

burner! The flames devour yards of linen and poplin suits, swiftly spreading to the flimsy one-sided facades of the set, which begin to crumble hazardously. People hindered by long flapping lab coats run hither and thither; stumble and crawl like ants. A tidal wave of blood, or Kool-Aid that looks and tastes like blood (new Blood-flavor Kool-Aid) rushes in, dousing the flames. As the actors splash and bob confusedly in the rising tide of sweet red beverage, tiny Sanrio characters appear paddling inflatable life rafts, still shaking off telltale staircase confetti of digitization. They save everybody. Except Thomas Dolby, that dork.

Optical: *To Shape the Future* ep (Metalheadz)

A back-and-forth slam, no hi-hat on earth ever sounded this gritty (except maybe on that Registrators single), but there's nothing macho or aggressive in its propulsive energy. The fantastic forward pressure of "Raging Calm" feels somehow geological: It could be six minutes or a million years. Either way, the depth and development of a sonic idea is exquisite.

Lysander Pearson: *Displacement* ep (Surface)

There's a lot to be said for music that doesn't do the things you like: If the only kind of country music you can appreciate is as raw and self-deprecating as those mopey-ass rock records at the bottom of the pile, maybe you're listening to the same thing in drag. Scarier to try liking a form of music for what it already is: Could I handle the mix of heart and treacle in a well-lubed '97 R&B song? I'm not saying you should, maybe you should run the other way—but touching stuff you think you don't like can be like feeling a strange animal, hoping it won't bite. Maybe it will nuzzle and lick you; maybe carry you off on huge rubbery wings and tickle you with long rubbery fingers. Oh, I'm thinking of nightgaunts. Anyhow, R&B usually sucks. But Techno and Jungle don't, and the parts that stay with me are always somehow hardcore; music that unhinges its jaw and opens wider and wider over the course of the song, or the beat, or whatever it is that happens until the shit drops off and changes completely. Lysander Pearson doesn't really do that here: While the beat on "exile" is strictly locked-groove (and sorta rubbery), "displacement's" hiccups and growls transform in that bouncy, driving way that makes windshield wipers in the rain a perennial classic. "belaté" isn't so much a dub *of* the previous song as the previous song *itself* with one of the knobs turned down, "displacement" bouncing off a distant wall. Tiny noises sneak into the corner of the frame and peek out then scamper away.

Registrators: "TV Hell" + "Vacation" one-sided 7" (Rip-Off)

Words spewed like bits of chewed food, hi-hat sounds like stereo amp crackle, these songs perform the subtle twist of cramming a dense five-minute Tex Avery cartoon down to ninety seconds. Um, probably the best live band on the planet too.

Shizuo: *Vs. Shizor* cd (Grand Royal)

Is *sarcasm* an accepted compositional technique? It is now, if the composers don't want their fucking asses kicked with what used to be called Drum 'n' Bass until Shizuo shat all over it. This record forgives you your trespasses. . . .

This Heat: *Made Available—John Peel Sessions* cd (These)

Post-rock. *Most* rock! Ghost rock. Prerock? Yup! This is dark, urgent music from another world that turns out to be ours. Unlike the welters of This Heat-inspired White Dub (sans Breadlocks) available, some kind of huge and rigorous spiritual force undergirds this music from 1977, probably This Heat's best and therefore as good a place as any to start if you wish to listen to a record. "The Fall of Saigon," a song about armchairs, living rooms, and a very hip ambassador's wife is what real Horror Rock would sound like: strings of ectoplasm, old newspapers, and a dream of revenge over a clanking beat. "You're only as good/as the words you understand/

AND YOU DON'T UNDERSTAND A THING." I feel like I'm playing drums when I listen to this, occasionally falling out of my seat.

Wu-Tang Clan: *Wu-Tang Forever* cd (does AOL have a record label?)

The most anticipated record of the summer might be remembered mostly for the record number of logos on the back (twelve, including Quicktime), because even the video game that came on the computer-ready cd sucked: It was like Quake, except instead of blowing people up you got to see more ads. It's not that the Wu-Tang Puppy Mill can't grind out music more striking than their t-shirts; RZA, Ol Dirty, and Gravediggaz prove it. But it's ridiculous the way critics, trying to still like hip-hop (and unable to listen to Mountain Boys or Witchboard 45s, I guess), have gone in for their identity shtick: Sasha Frere-Jones, quick to see through hate-fuck rockers Pussy Galore as a classic white quest for authenticity, flops over on his back for these guys: "Why buy an album that's obviously too long, too expensive, and half of which could be lost forever with no harm done? Because it's the Wu. . . ."

Huh. As Kool Keith said, "Keep it real, represent WHAT? My nuts." Now that the Clan is giving more exciting interviews than shows, tossing promotional squeeze bottles out in front of a Staten Island version of *La Bohème*, and totally unsubstantiated rumors of a failed promo track are spreading ("Wu-Tang Clan drinks nuttin' but Mountain Dew," canned when the agency saw what happened to Ice Cube's Tab cameo: "Tab—wastin' all the sucka soda pops/load up the clip and watch the wack drinks drop!"), the backlash is probably next—right after the Nike uprising.

Reissues

However appropriate last summer's waves of public outrage at HarperCollins' mass cancellation of some one hundred book contracts, it tended to obscure the far more frequent and much less publicized fact that important books are routinely put out of print by publishers who deem their annual sales too low, too slow, or both. Luckily, what seems anemic to the *Oprah*-addled CFO at one house is "steady backlist" to the vigilant editor elsewhere, and thanks to these brave scavengers a number of important works remain in print.

The best of the reissue crop this fall is surely E.B. White's famous collection of essays, *One Man's Meat* (Tilbury House, $14.95 paperback). Originally published in 1942, the book began as a series of pieces in *Harper's Magazine* documenting White's removal from New York City to a saltwater farm in Maine. (That ancient connection with HarperCollins, of course, did not keep Murdoch's boys from putting the book out of print.) Though White is often cast as the poster-boy for the Personal Essay and the memoirist's memoirist, he deserves far better. His finest qualities are on display in *One Man's Meat*—the great precision and casual warmth of his prose; his pleasure in the minutiae of daily life; and his cheerful, bitter iconoclasm.

In all of these respects he resembles George Orwell (no doubt to the displeasure of the many who still confuse *Charlotte's Web* with *Animal Farm*). There's no question that Orwell was able to weave his experience into more complex tangles and to avoid the syrupy tone and silly epigrams ("Diplomacy is the lowest form of politeness because it misquotes the greatest number of people") that occasionally mar White's style. But White, born like Orwell at the turn of the century, shared much of the literary upbringing of the Lost Generation, and his modernist sense of the telling detail seems straight out of Hemingway's *In Our Time*. He writes, for example, of "the elevator boy in my hotel [who] after he has shut the grilled gate and started the car, always slips his hand through the bars of the gate so that as he passes each floor the sill-plate will give him a dangerous little kiss on the end of his finger. It is the only record he keeps of his fabulous travels." And in the commercial chatter of American culture he recognizes greater truths than in conventional faiths:

> Some day, if I ever get around to it, I would like to write the definitive review of America's most fascinating book, the Sears Roebuck catalogue. It is a monumental volume, and in many households is a more powerful document than the Bible.

Written during the Second World War, *One Man's Meat* is also an oblique chronicle of the war years' effects on American civilian life. While some of White's mushy reflections on liberty have only grown even mushier with age, his wry commentary on the tenor of the times—from the swiftly changing landscape to the follies of the World's Fair of 1939 and the traumas of a nation preparing for war ("Blackout curtains are up at the kitchen windows, wild cucumber up at the kitchen door")—is fascinating. His remarkable story about the moment he and his wife heard about the bombing of Pearl Harbor is a case in point:

> How quickly life's accents shifted on that sudden and unforgettable Sunday—the fateful seventh of December. My wife was getting a hot-water bag for somebody, and somehow she managed to lose the stopper down the toilet, beyond recall. This grotesque little incident seemed to upset her to a disproportionate degree: it was because she felt that, now that the war had begun in earnest, there was no excuse for any clumsiness in home nursing. The loss of the stopper suddenly seemed as severe a blow as the loss of a battleship. Life, which for two years had had a rather dreamlike quality, came instantly into sharp focus. The time for losing hot-water bag stoppers was over and gone.

But the most extraordinary pieces in the book are two essays in the form of lists: "Report" from 1939 and "Memorandum" from 1941. These are the kind of writing you turn to when all else is in doubt; the latter is even worthy of joining William Gass's pantheon of great literary lists (see his hilarious essay, "I've Got a Little List"). True to Montaigne's spirit to his last, White's subject is the only subject: "The first person singular is the only grammatical instrument I am able to use without cutting myself." (Tilbury House Publishers, 132 Water Street, Gardiner, Maine 04345).

Though not strictly a "reissue," since the stories have never appeared in book form before, *If I Were Boss: The Early Business Stories of Sinclair Lewis* (edited by Anthony Di Renzo, Southern Illinois University Press, $19.95 paperback) is simply too important a reclamation project to ignore. Written between 1915 and 1921—the time of *Main Street* and *Babbitt*—the fifteen stories here capture the mind of modern American business at its point of origin, epitomized by figures like Mr. Small in "Commutation: $9.17": he was "neither

meek and meeching nor tall and pompous. He was neither young nor old, bearded nor clean-shaven. Even other commuters remarked that he looked like a commuter. . . . His face was medium looking. He was medium sized. He was medium."

Like H.L. Mencken, Lewis shuddered at the American tendency to celebrate mediocrity, and these stories reveal the full depth of his revulsion. Together his stories and novels of this period form a remarkably Dickensian portrait of aspiration and banality; roll them all in one great ball and you get the American *Pickwick Papers*. But fun as the stories are to read, with their mild surprise endings and light screwball moments, Lewis (as DiRenzo astutely points out) "mines the collective hallucinations of the working middle class," and you're left with perhaps the best document of what Sherwood Anderson called the "mad awakening" of the early twentieth century. (Southern Illinois University Press, P.O. Box 3697 Carbondale, Illinois 62902-3697)

Regular readers of these pages will not be surprised to learn of the gladness in Baffler offices upon the reissue of John Dos Passos's *U.S.A.* (Modern Library, $40.00 hardcover). Other notable reissues appearing this fall include a 25th anniversary edition of Jeremy Brecher's *Strike!* (South End Press, $22.00 paperback); John O'Hara's late, bitter portrait of ambition in Hollywood, *The Big Laugh* (Ecco Press, $14.95 paperback); and Brendan Gill's fun-for-all-ages *Here at The New Yorker* (Da Capo, $15.95 paperback). One reissue that won't be showing up in many American bookstores, but is well worth seeking out, is Ian's Jack's *Before the Oil Ran Out* (Vintage Books), an elegant and scathing chronicle of the eighties matched only by Christopher Hitchens at his best. Jack was hailed some time ago as the "finest feature writer at work in Britain," and once you read the lead piece—"Finished With Engines," about his father and his own childhood in Scotland in the fifties—you'll know why. Three pillars of social science also make their return this year: Daniel Bell's *Cultural Contradic-*

tions of Capitalism (Basic Books, $15.00 paperback); Richard Titmuss's *The Gift Relationship* (The New Press, $30.00 hardcover); and Walter Lippman's classic *Public Opinion* is also back in print (The Free Press, $13.00 paperback). On the last, we'll stick with Mencken's assessment that "what Lippmann tried to do as a professor, laboriously and without imagination, Sinclair Lewis [did] as an artist with a few vivid strokes."

—Pepper Callicles

Category Killers

"Life," says Chad—*of course* his name is Chad—"Life," says he, "is for the taking." If you didn't see *In the Company of Men*, the drama of corporate advancement where Chad utters this immortal *double-entendre*, and if you don't believe me that he says it, pick up any of the workplace murder mysteries being published this fall: They all seem to think Chad's the culture-king in these parts; they all take Chad's phrase as the credo of the age. Yes! Life *is* for the taking! What *defines* the new genre of "downsizing" fiction, it seems, is the angry guy who takes a lifetime of Chadisms seriously, who honestly believes he is a class-A, one hundred and ten percent-giving, helmet-strapped-on-and-game-fully-entered, positive-thinking, no-not-just-positive-thinking-but-positive-*envisioning*, opportunity-devouring, doing-it-even-before-it's-a-good-idea, ass-kicking motherfucker who's just been "downsized" from his job (another element is rage against the lily-livered politically-correct castrati who invent these hated euphemisms: Back in Chad's dad's day they just called it "getting fired," or "getting canned," or "getting the heave-ho" or "getting the sack" or "getting your ass handed to you" or "getting the old nuts torn off") and who decides he's going to take this downsizing as the long-awaited opportunity to do a little entrepreneurship on his own, you know, working out of his house, investing in all sorts of risk-embracing equipment, diving headlong the kind of entrepreneurship he's learned about from gangster movies, or from serial-killer movies, or from

trashy fiction like this shit. So instead of *competing* with the other guys, he just *kills* 'em, get it?

Donald Westlake knows full well that, once upon a time, they called this process "getting the ax," and his office mystery, bearing the admirably direct title *The Ax* (Mysterious Press, $23.00 hardcore), features the flashily and suggestively named protoganist "Burke Devore" (just let that one roll off your tongue a couple of times: "Burke Devore! Burke fuckin' Devore! How ya been, ya goddam dee-vore!") who's been "downsized" by the—check out the irony!—*Halcyon* Mills Paper Company. Burke, a fully empowered paper industry management professional, is not only *fired*, he's *fired up*, and he takes what you might call an *aggressively hands-on* approach to his job search—his hands filled with none other than one of those sharp righteous heavy steel-and-hickory devices we call an "ax." This is hardly the first clever and compelling ironic twist to which we clever readers are treated in Westlake's *tour de force*, though: Devore actually uses fake job announcents to collect the resumes of all the other hapless "downsized" drones in his management category, whom he then hunts down and treats to a second helping of "ax."

Q: So does Burke ever get around to killing the guy who fired him?

A: Hell no! A good bourgeois to the last, he imagines his murder spree as a sort of job-search with weapons, a matter of presenting yourself as the best available candidate ("available" being the key word here).

Q: So what happens with Burke's wife?

A: She splits!

———————

William Heffernan gives his hero the slightly beefier, manlier name "Jack Fallon" and has him hail from an older generation of management professionals, Nam-hardened guys who wouldn't take a piss in the woods with one these modern "downsizers." In Heffernan's new mystery, *The Dinosaur Club* (which William Morrow, $24.00 hardcover, is cleverly trying to sell as a manifesto of popular resistance to the terror of "downsizing"), the action never gets so out of hand that Jack gets the sack . . . no, no, no . . . Jack has seen through the "downsizers' " plots, and he's got together with a couple of other senior management professionals and organized a clandestine group for workplace struggle (hmmm . . . what does that remind me of?); and as it turns out, Jack's the boy *doing* the sacking—in more ways than one (and not counting moonlighting [to—ahem—*collect valuable market-research data*] in the checkout line at the local Piggly Wiggly)! But Jack's troubles are even more vexing than Burke's. If he loses the battle with the "downsizers," it's his kids' Ivy League educations that are on the line, slated for termination; Jack's bosses know it: they've driven Jack up—not against a wall, as Jack himself would have done back in the day—but to the edge of the crevasse, the bottomless black hole of class; they're holding Jack's head over it so he can get a good whiff of all the chumps left behind while the company's assets appreciated so outstandingly the last few years, so he can see them all staring dully at their TVs and dragging themselves to their jobs at Orange Julius, get a good picture of the social annihilation that befalls the "downsized," can realize that if he muffs this one, the Fallons are trailer-park people for the next two generations.

Q: Is Jack's wife true and faithful in his hour of need?

A: Of course not!

Q: Does Jack get laid by a pretty female anyway?

A: Shitchyeah!

Q: Is his antagonist a hated WASP?

A: You better believe it. Bearing the effete name, "Carter Bennet," this elitist would-be downsizer has no qualms about sending our Celtic he-man protagonist spinning off into the hell of downward mobility. Just to underscore how unrelentingly *ee-vill* Bennet is, Heffernan embroils him in one of those sick and wrong love joneses with a close relative that rich and polished folks are supposed to have.

Q: So do Jack's kids become crackers?

A: You'll have to read it to find out.

—Owen Hatteras

Somewhere in France

Lydie Salvayre's *The Award* (Trans. Jane Davey, Four Walls, Eight Windows, $18.00 hardcover) is an odd company farce that takes an awards ceremony for longtime employees as its narrative conceit. Set in a French automobile factory, the book consists of introductory speeches by executives and then responses by the honored employee winners. What's interesting about the exchange is that the executives' speeches are really propagandistic excursions on the greatness of the company, with only small mention of the actual employee; the employee responses, meanwhile, are often accounts of bestial working conditions or deeply pessimistic commentaries on life. When one worker finishes his speech by saying "I only hope I can hang on till retirement," the company higher-up replies with, "As he so nicely pointed out in his charming speech, our factory wouldn't be what it is today without the dynamic presence of our Division Heads." *The Award* lampoons the utter lack of communication in inter-office communication, as well as certain precepts of management gurus ("Work yourselves to death without anyone ordering you to. Simply tell yourselves that you are your own foreman"). But it has a strangely anachronistic view of working life. Perhaps this is because it was published in France in 1993, before American-style restructuring began in Europe; perhaps it is world-historical nostalgia on the part of the author (billed as the daughter of "an anarchist mother and a communist father"). Whatever the reason, *The Award* reads as a kind of dated absurdist drama, viewing corporations as the agents of hyper-paternalism and Orwellian control, and workers as a rebellious, collectivized mob pacified by doublespeak. Its weaknesses, though, point up the strangest aspects of the corporate age in which we live now: Companies rule the world but no one fears that the bonds of an employer are too strong; control comes not from a martinet boss but begins with the self-empowered individual.

—Tom Vanderbilt

REMAINDER TABLE

ROBERT NEDELKOFF

Pamela Moore Plus Forty

One afternoon toward the end of 1982 I happened across a trade paperback called *The Catalog of Cool,* compiled by a veteran music-industry publicist named Gene Sculatti. The book consisted of articles and blurbs by Sculatti and his cronies, among whom were some names—Ronn Spencer and Davin Seay, for example—familiar only to steady readers of music magazines, and a handful of names—Nick Tosches and Richard Meltzer—known in slightly wider circles. The book represented an early attempt to codify that species of 1950s bachelor-pad nostalgia that would finally catch on among "twentysomethings" more than a decade later, with heavy coverage given to Terry Southern, Frank Sinatra's Rat Pack, Louis Prima, Robert Mitchum and others. Garage bands of the 1960s, Harvey Pekar's *American Splendor,* and some other things only tangentially related to the 1950-63 archetype of "cool" were also included. One sixteen-page section summarized a few dozen essential "reads" for the aspiring hepster, including some obvious choices, like Richard Farina's *Been Down So Long* and the works of Nelson Algren; some selections a little ahead of their time for 1982, like Jim Thompson's *The Killer Inside Me;* some books by authors I'd heard of before, like Chandler Brossard and Bernard Wolfe; and one book by an author of whom I had never heard:

Chocolates For Breakfast, by Pamela Moore (Holt, Rinehart & Winston hardcover; Bantam paperback): This eighteen-year-old "answer to Françoise Sagan" penned the ultimate teen sophisticate fantasy in '56. Her 15-year-old heroine first balls a fag actor in H'wood, then makes it with some hermetic, filthy rich, hotel-bound Italian count in NY, where she's gone to swing at the Stork Club. At home, mom serves martinis at 11, breakfast at noon.

I noted the blurb and read on, assuming I would encounter Pamela Moore's name elsewhere. I never did. Several years later, on a whim, I pulled down *Contemporary Authors* and found an entry for her in Vols. 1-4, revised. The sketchy story it told was of interest, but I did not look into it further.

The eighties rolled on. By the end of 1984, the success of Jay McInerney, Bret Easton Ellis, and Tama Janowitz had gotten the media talking about "young writers" and hailing the escapades of a bogus literary school called the "Brat Pack." Reviewers and gossip columnists pondered which member of the gang would be the "new Salinger," which chronicle of youthful anomie would turn out to be the authentic successor of *Catcher in the Rye.* Before long, though, it was clear that those anxious to discover another Salinger would do better to look backward.

In 1992, I encountered the work of Mary Maclane, the Montana-bred novelist whose work caused a sensation in Teddy Roosevelt's America and whose vogue vanished as quickly as it had come, leaving her to die in obscurity in Chicago a quarter-century later. (The opening words of her first and best-known book were reprinted in the front section of the November 1994 *Harper's;* the book as a whole was included in the 1993 anthology *Tender Darkness.*) The episode made me recall the mysterious Pamela Moore, and after years of searching I was able to find copies of all four of her novels in a dusty warehouse answering to the name of bookstore just south of Oakland. I have also sifted through what facts of her life I could learn from the pages of old magazines and newspapers. The story I have compiled from them follows.

I.

In the summer of 1956, the hottest thing going in American fiction publishing—as in the publishing industries of Western Europe and England—was the *oeuvre* of a 21-year-old Frenchwoman named Françoise Sagan. Her first book, *Bonjour Tristesse,* written at the age of eighteen, had caused a sensation in her native land in 1954 and had shortly been translated into English, climbing the American and British bestseller lists with ease in 1955, settling in at number one and making the title such a catchphrase that not even Hollywood could bring itself to change the moniker of the movie version to *Goodbye Sorrow* or even *Bye Bye Blues.*

During that summer it was clear that Sagan's second book, *Une Certaine Sourire,* would do even better, as it piled up the largest advance sale for its publisher, E.P. Dutton, since the twenties. American houses, agog at the figures, were conducting an intense search for the domestic equivalent of the free-spirited writer famed for driving a sports car barefoot. Such a writer, given that her subject matter would be the problems and pleasures of youth, could also count on comparisons to J.D. Salinger, whose following had only just begun to exceed "cult" status. (It was in this year that the first censorship fracas involving *The Catcher In The Rye* erupted when a college professor was dismissed

for assigning it to his students.)

It fell to Rinehart & Co., publishers of Norman Mailer's first two books, to find the American Sagan. She turned out to be the obligatory eighteen years of age—her book, in fact, came out three weeks before her nineteenth birthday. She was precocious in other ways as well, being a *senior* in college when the book came out, and having entered the world of higher education a month shy of sixteen. Her academic areas of interest, rather than the expected English and "creative writing," were ancient and medieval history (with emphasis on military history) and, for her minors, Roman Law and Greek—with straight A's in all of them. She had acted in summer stock, and, as the daughter of a magazine editor, could be expected to handle publicity with aplomb. Her college, Barnard, struck the right note of elitist bohemia. Best of all, her book was set in the world of the rich, spoiled haute monde—what had been called "Café Society" in the thirties, and which had only just acquired the title "Jet Set." Her name was Pamela Moore, and her book was *Chocolates For Breakfast.*

Pamela was born on September 22, 1937, in New York, the daughter of two writers. Her father, Don Moore, was 32 at the time. He was the son of an Iowa newspaper publisher; in 1925, he had graduated second in his class at Dartmouth. In the late twenties he had edited Edgar Rice Burroughs and other pulp writers at the *Argosy All Story Weekly,* then signed on with Hearst's King Features Syndicate as writer for a new comic strip drawn by Alex Raymond (who'd just finished doing a G-man strip written by Dashiell Hammett). The strip was *Flash Gordon,* and Moore wrote it, as well as *Jungle Jim,* until 1954, with time out for trips to Hollywood to work on the serial versions of the two strips.

Sometime in the early thirties, Don Moore married a young woman named Isabel Walsh. She already had a daughter, Elaine, who took her stepfather's name. Isabel was a writer as well, specializing in syrupy women's-magazine stories, and soon had work published in

Redbook, Hearst's *American Weekly,* and *Cosmopolitan.* For Rinehart, her daughter's future publisher, she wrote three novels in the early forties, with titles like *The Other Woman* and *I'll Never Let You Go.* About then Don and Isabel Moore split up. In later years Isabel devoted herself to supervising the show-horse riding career of her daughter Elaine, who won a number of championships in the forties before retiring to marry and settle in Florida. Pamela shuttled back and forth between parents: her mother in New York, where Isabel edited *Photoplay* for some years; her father, mostly in Hollywood, where he supplemented his King Features earnings by working as a story editor for RKO and Warner Brothers. Both of Pamela's parents moved in a world defined by Hedda Hopper and Louella Parsons on one coast, and by Walter Winchell on the other. It was a world where childhood had to be cultivated like an orchid in a greenhouse if it was to happen at all. For Pamela Moore the situation was a tragic one: Childhood succeeded maturity, rather than preceding it. One of the most poignant aspects of her first novel, in fact, is the curious perspective of age with which the narrator describes her protagonist: "Years later, Courtney would remember . . ." or "As a grown woman, Courtney would realize . . . ." The writer of the book herself was eighteen; the character ages from fifteen to sixteen in the book's course. Through the fictive and narrative personas of her first novel, Pamela Moore repeats this pathetic plea: *I don't understand how one endures these things now, but one day, when I'm older and wiser . . . .* Her subsequent books show how far she was from ever reaching that status, as woman or writer.

II.

Rinehart, as noted, snapped up *Chocolates For Breakfast,* and, following a careful publicity campaign, unleashed it on the world in September 1956. It attracted attention at once, and no wonder. The first chapter depicts Courtney Farrell, the heroine, and Janet Parker, her best friend, sitting in their prep school dorm—in Janet's case, "with her clothes off" (as the novel's second paragraph pointedly informs the reader)—while arguing over whether Courtney is stumbling into a lesbian relationship with her English teacher. Before many pages have passed, Courtney is attempting to lose her virginity to a pretty-boy acquaintance of her fading movie-star mother at the Garden of Allah in Hollywood, the one-time home of F. Scott Fitzgerald, as Pamela notes in the book. True, Moore does prudently postpone the virginity-losing until Courtney has safely reached sixteen, but the book's impact was still enormous, given the moral climate of 1956 (the Legion of Decency condemned *Baby Doll* the same year, there were whisperings about a reputedly pornographic paperback from Paris labeled *Lolita,* and Otto Preminger was refused an MPAA certificate for the use of the word "virgin" in *The Moon Is Blue*).

"Not very long ago, it would have been regarded as shocking to find girls in their teens *reading* the kind of books they're now writing," wrote Robert Clurman in *The New York Times Book Review*—and that was *before* publication. *Newsweek's* reviewer, all too prescient, wrote: "She may well be also a part of a trend among publishers to start a new cycle of youth problem novels, as told by the young—a kind of literary parallel to the more overt delinquencies of the switch-blade hoodlums."

The novel went into two printings before publication, and scraped onto the bottom of the hardcover bestseller lists for several weeks in September and October. The comparisons to Françoise Sagan continued, though William Hogan of the *San Francisco Chronicle* noted that Pamela's "dabblings" in sex were not as "blatant" as the French writer's. He also remarked: "It would appear that Miss Moore had hoped . . . to become the female J.D. Salinger." The comparison has been made countless times since, for countless writers, but this was one of the first instances.

In the weeks prior to the appearance

of her book, Moore had, in Salingerian fashion, made herself unavailable for interviews. Instead, she busied herself studying the "strategy and tactics" of European warfare in a tour of battlefields, which fact struck the journalists of the time as an entertaining eccentricity in a young woman. But after publication, she juggled the studies of her final year at Barnard with being, in her words, "caught between the American public and journalists who wanted to know about my love life, and my college friends studying creative writing who condemned me as 'commercial.' " She often made the gossip columns when she ventured to the theater or a restaurant. Publishers were deluged with manuscripts by young women seeking to imitate her, as she had been thought to be imitating Sagan (although the Fitzgerald of *This Side of Paradise* was clearly her most important model). As much as the best-known of her counterparts in the eighties, she was a star. And, all over the country, young mothers and fathers began naming their daughters Courtney.

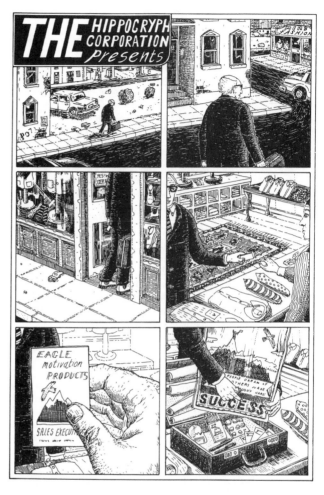

It seems worthwhile to note here that Pamela Moore's one permanent contribution to American culture was in the area of nomenclature. In all the half-dozen "How to Name Your Baby" books published before 1960 that I've seen, "Courtney" appears exclusively as a male name of French origin. Prior to 1956, it was a fairly common Christian name for men in England and the Southern United States. Every female "Courtney" that this writer has personally known, in fact, was born in 1958 or in a subsequent year—that is, during or immediately after the period that *Chocolates* began to sell in paperback.

When in high school and college I encountered a number of Courtneys born in 1958 through 1960; thereafter, for four years—the period the book was out of print—the name appears to have dropped off in frequency, then reappeared with a vengeance in 1964, the year *Chocolates* reappeared in print. The name has maintained its popularity since then, as a star of the nation's most popular sitcom and one of this mighty land's twenty-five most influential citizens (if *Time* be trusted) can respectively attest. The *Guinness Book of Names*, in fact, includes a survey showing that through the nineties "Courtney" has consistently ranked among the twenty names most frequently given female infants in the United States.

Pamela Moore's reaction to her stardom, upon graduating in May 1957, was (quoting from her *Contemporary Authors* sketch) to "expatriate to Paris to find my identity." A month later, Bantam issued *Chocolates* in paperback. That edition sold 600,000 copies in the last six months of the year, and would have consolidated Moore's celebrity if she had stayed in America. (Another thing that would have consolidated her fame would have been a movie version of the book, but no such movie was made, undoubtedly because the moguls viewed her picture of Hollywood in much the same light as they regarded the depictions offered by Budd Schulberg, Horace McCoy, or Nathanael West.) Pamela's reasons for going to Europe were clear. Like the heroine of her book, she wanted to be taken seriously, not only as a writer, but as a person. In an America where the burgeoning cult of the nymphet was shortly to make a millionaire of an obscure Cornell professor, she was clearly not going to be allowed to grow up easily. Things were different in Europe. There, *Chocolates For Breakfast* not only made the bestseller lists but was favorably reviewed in both Italy and France, whose pundits warmed unexpectedly to a novel which was ostensibly an imitation of one of their own writers. In America, the public wanted to know about her boyfriends and eating habits; "in Paris," Pamela Moore observed, "they wanted to know my politics and metaphysics."

Her timing was fortuitous; the first stirrings of the Beat movement, in the form of "Howl," *On The Road,* and contraband chapters of *Naked Lunch,* were already before the public, and the "alternative" culture that continues to beguile aging columnists and sell running shoes was in its nascent stages. In Europe, Pamela Moore was perceived as a part of this culture. She spent the next year explaining herself on radio and television in France and Italy. She was even listed in a multivolume literary encyclopedia

published by the prestigious Milan house of Mondadori in 1961. The entry includes a photograph of her posing in what must have been a European TV producer's idea of a Greenwich Village coffeehouse, complete with guitarist, mazes of cigarette smoke, flattened paperbacks, and black-clad denizens.

In the spring of 1958, she returned to America. But she was not interested in resuming her career as a celebrity. She got married instead. Her husband, Adam Kanarek, was of Polish origin, and had very little in common with the people of Beverly Hills, the Westchester horse set, the habitués of "21" or the Stork Club, or any other world Pamela had encountered. The couple settled down in New York, and he was soon attending law school.

Meanwhile, Pamela's parents continued their literary labors. Don Moore published his only book, *The Naked Warriors,* about Navy frogmen, in 1956. And Isabel Moore began publishing novels again, with paperback houses—most notably (under the name Elaine Dorian) *The Sex Cure,* a version of *Peyton Place* set in Cooperstown, New York, her residence at the time. The book inspired her famously image-conscious neighbors to daub her house with paint. Isabel also studied for a Ph.D. at Columbia, traveled in Russia, and wrote, in 1961, *The Day The Communists Took Over America,* which, despite its Red Scare title and semi-pulp style, is an unexpectedly sophisticated treatment of a resurgent Klan and neo-Nazis stirring up homegrown genocide.

By early 1959 Pamela, with her husband's encouragement, had resumed writing. She completed her second novel quickly; the use of a diary in the book's final pages suggests one source for her facility as a stylist. It was submitted to American publishers and rejected—not surprising, since, in terms of theme, style, and characterization, it was very different from *Chocolates,* and none but the most understanding of publishers and editors are keen on such a step from a writer, especially when the earlier book has been the bonanza that

Pamela's was. Instead, it was issued by her French publisher, Juilliard, as *Les Pigeons de Saint Marc* in 1960, and as *East Side Story* by Longmans in the U.K. in 1961. The reviews were still favorable in France; in England, the book received a one-paragraph notice in the *Times Literary Supplement,* a journal where *Chocolates* had been reviewed at some length. When *Chocolates'* paperback sales began to slacken in America by the end of 1960, the awful truth was clear: Pamela Moore, a few months past twenty-three, was a has-been, as completely a relic of an era as coonskin caps or prime-time quiz shows.

Still, she was a writer, so she kept on writing. In 1962, *L'Exil de Suzy-Coeur* appeared, only in France, and she gave some interviews to *Paris-Match* and *Le Figaro Littéraire* that spring. Soon after this came what must have been hopeful news: Simon & Schuster accepted her fourth book, *The Horsy Set.* At the very end of the year she became pregnant. Things were going well, and given that Pamela Moore appears to have been suffering from bipo-

lar disorder (her description of her heroine Courtney's mood swings in *Chocolates* is sufficiently precise that a modern-day psychiatrist reading the book would hardly refrain from an impromptu diagnosis), it would have been preferable for things to stay that way, given the absence of meaningful therapy for such a condition in that era.

But things did not continue to go well. *The Horsy Set,* a story set in the wealthy, decadent world of show-horse racing in which her sister was such a prominent figure, received no notice in *The New York Times,* nor in any of the major newsmagazines or literary and cultural weeklies. What few reviews it received appeared in daily papers in those cities on the Gulf and Atlantic coastlines where show-horses were big news, presumably to let the locals know that they might figure as characters in a book. Almost no public libraries ordered the book, and hardcover sales were minimal. Dell issued a paperback *Horsy Set* in 1963, in what must have been a large printing—copies of it are almost as easy to find as *Chocolates*. But that one printing remained in stock for nearly five years. Years later Doubleday reprinted it, bound with a war novel by another writer, as part of a series called "Stories for Men." Pamela's bid for recognition as a serious writer had failed utterly; the publication of her third novel as *The Exile of Suzy-Q* in March 1964 by the second-rate house, Paperback Library, served only to underline the fact. (No copy of this book is even in the Library of Congress.) The birth of a son, Kevin, in September 1963, and her husband's admission to the bar were all the compensation for this misfortune that she would receive.

She kept writing. Her fifth novel was tentatively titled *Kathy.* Its protagonist was a washed-up writer, contemplating her failure. Pamela's model, F. Scott Fitzgerald, had taken sixteen years to travel the path from *This Side of Paradise* to "The Crack-Up;" she had covered the distance in less than half that time. Through the early months of 1964, as *Chocolates* was reissued and as stray readers in news shops and drugstores discovered she had some new books, she continued to work. One of the characters in her novel, according to Detective Robert Gosselin of the NYPD, "talked about marital difficulties and suicidal tendencies . . . there was a reference to that guy Hemingway and how he died."

On Sunday, June 7, 1964, she reached the end of the line.

It was late afternoon. Her husband was out of the apartment. Her baby was asleep in the bedroom. She sat in the living room, at her desk, and wrote in her diary. "If you put it all together," Detective Gosselin told the press the following day, "the last four pages, under the date June 7, indicate that she was having trouble with her writing and intended to destroy herself." He said that the pages described the rifle barrel feeling "cold and alien" in her mouth, and continued: "She wanted the last four pages, the suicide note, added to the novel she was working on."

Pamela Moore finished writing, inserted a .22 caliber rifle into her mouth, and pulled the trigger. Her husband found her on the living-room floor. She was three months short of twenty-seven.

III.

Kathy was never published. In September, Dell issued her second novel under the title of *Diana;* both it and *Suzy-Q* were out of print by the end of the year. Bantam reprinted *Chocolates* thrice more; it went out of print in America for the last time at the end of 1967, about when Dell pulped its last copies of *The Horsy Set* and not long after what would have been Pamela Moore's thirtieth birthday. In England and Europe, her books stayed in print until a little after the turn of the decade.

Since then, her work has never been reprinted. Apart from the 1982 reference that had first drawn my attention, the *Contemporary Authors* sketch (last updated in 1968), and an entry in *Who's Who of American Women* for 1965-66 (apparently compiled before her death), her name appears in almost no books or reference materials. She has been the subject of no articles since the newspaper stories immediately following her suicide. Nor does she figure in any academic discussions of feminist literature, despite the fact that some of her work clearly prefigures the great awakening of feminism in the late sixties and seventies.

Don Moore, her father, was "rediscovered" when the movie version of *Flash Gordon* came out in 1980, and he colorfully recounted his years on the strip and in Hollywood for movie and science-fiction magazines that year. He didn't discuss Pamela. He died in Florida in 1986.

Isabel Moore continued to write. In 1965, under the pseudonym of Grace Walker, she published a biography of her surviving daughter, the full title of which is: *Elaine Moore Moffat, Blue Ribbon Horsewoman: The Complete Life Story of a Champion Rider Who Learned to Deal with Life by Learning to Deal with Horses.* Two years later, she published *Women of the Green Cafe,* a paperback novel about lesbians which was characterized in the leading bibliography of lesbian fiction as "exploitative." In 1970, she published *That Summer In Connecticut,* a smoothly written but cliché-riddled account of a May-December romance that indicates just what difficulty she must have had understanding her younger daughter given the generational gulf that separated the women who came of age before the fifties and those who matured just as the implications of *The Second Sex* were beginning to resonate in this country.

IV.

Chocolates For Breakfast begins with the protagonist, Courtney Farrell—described as a "slim, dark-haired girl of fifteen" with "green, large, rebellious eyes"—sitting in her dormitory at the exclusive, all-female Scaisbrooke Hall, arguing with her equally rebellious, pre-debutante friend, Janet Parker, over whether her crush on her English teacher is developing into something beyond a schoolgirl infatuation. Janet, while discussing Courtney's dilemma, eats a banana; a later chapter, in which Courtney visits a psychiatrist under the school's auspices, features enough Freudian jargon to establish that the symbolism is conscious and that Pamela Moore understood earlier than some of her contemporaries the inadequacies of orthodox Freudianism to explain the inner world of women.

Courtney is unable to interact very well with any of her teachers except the aforementioned English instructor, Miss Rosen, who informs her that they can no longer see that much of each other anymore; this well-handled scene was probably what earned the novel a positive citation in the aforementioned bibliography of lesbian-themed fiction. Nor does Courtney get along with any of her fellow students, save Janet. The reason is simple: Courtney, the daughter of divorced parents, does not come from the well-heeled background of her peers. Her father, who is "in publishing," is a nebulous and ineffectual-seeming character, none too definite a presence in the book. Her mother, Sondra, with whom Courtney lives, is a once-popular movie actress now on the skids. Courtney's classmates are interested in her only to the extent that she has gossip to relay about Cary Grant or Tyrone Power. And after a trip to the shrink, the school sends her home for the summer, "home" being her mother's apartment at the Garden of Allah on the Sunset Strip, in what is now West Hollywood. All of this action, like that of her later book *The*

Horsy Set, is set in 1953, a year that bore some obscure significance for Pamela Moore: The Korean War had just ended, Eisenhower was in the Oval Office, Stalin had just died, and Joe McCarthy's influence had just peaked.

The chapters detailing life at the Garden, and at the small apartment in a déclassé section of Beverly Hills to which Courtney and her mother move after Sondra's finances no longer permit the hotel, are the most observant and entertaining in the book, though the subject matter itself is downbeat. Here Courtney meets Barry Cabot, a friend of her mother's and a onetime bobbysoxers' favorite now debilitated by alcohol and shame about his bisexuality. Courtney immediately takes a shine to Barry, but the consummation of their relationship must wait until after she's sixteen, by which time she's enrolled at Beverly Hills High and has discovered that she has even less in common with the forebears of Dylan, Brenda, and Donna than she did with the finishing school crowd.

So Courtney goes to Schwab's Drugstore, her old spot for trysts with Barry, where she finds the actor and decides that there are now no obstacles to . . .

> Love. She had not known what it could be, and she would never live without it again. She had not known that she would know so much about love, the first time . . . she could never see life as she had seen it before, life with an entire sphere dimly seen.

Before the reader clucks at the evident influence of Pamela's mother's *Redbook* stories on her literary style, it should be noted that the passage—and the book itself—is still struggling with the mores of the prefeminist era. Whenever Courtney becomes really dissatisfied with the world around her, she thinks to herself that she wouldn't have these problems if she were a man—which may explain her male name. She thinks of her mother's career as an actress, for example, not as an achievement, but as training acquired in Sondra's youth not so much to build a career as to land a rich husband, and which is now to be used only because things didn't work out

with the husband. The novel itself proceeds to lead Courtney almost ironically towards the same dilemma: Can she or can she not acquire an affluent, ambitious husband? Pamela Moore is writing a *Bildungsroman* in a familiar tradition, but where a male protagonist would "find himself," Courtney ends up finding someone to whom she can subsume her identity—a familiar convention in romance fiction as it has developed from *Jane Eyre*, but disturbing to encounter in a book otherwise the product of a fairly powerful individual sensibility.

But, before all of this comes to pass, the book's second part closes with Courtney attempting suicide, her affair with Barry frustrated by the reappearance of his male lover, a character whose sympathetic portrayal contrasts with the homophobia with which male authors of the period—even one of the stature of William Gaddis (as *The Recognitions'* party scenes show)—would have treated him. Following a stay in a sanitarium (not depicted in the book), Courtney and her mother move back to New York, where Sondra pursues TV work and Courtney renews her friendship with Janet Parker, now expelled from Scaisbrooke and living with her father, an alcoholic Wall Street broker.

The daily routine of the two friends consists of endless evenings at the Stork Club (referred to as "the Bird"); P.J. Clarke's is once suggested as an alternate hangout. Janet and Courtney also crash parties on Long Island, in the company of lads recently suspended from Harvard or Yale for drinking or violating curfew. Before long, Courtney is introduced to an old flame of Janet's, Anthony Neville, a world-weary product of Boston Brahminism and old Italian aristocracy who affects a rather different persona from that of the fallen Ivy Leaguers:

> "I've been writing a story," [Anthony] announced. "It's about two Lesbians who are married by a homosexual priest—"
> He paused and looked at Courtney.
> "You're Catholic, of course." She nodded.
> "—by a homosexual priest in a terribly floral ceremony in Switzerland. Up to

this point they have been living quite happily in sin, but now their idyll has been destroyed . . ."

Moore uses this touch of decadent Europe in the same manner as Henry James in his early works: to provide a foil for the clean-cut, upright American who will soon show up and do what the enervated preppies (all far more interested in drinking than sex) are unable to do. After Anthony has spirited Courtney to places like Chambord and the Hotel Pierre and told her precious parables about how she has lifted his blague, the responsible life appears in the person of Charles Cunningham, the son of a Boston lawyer who lost his allowance when he was suspended from Yale for drunkenness. Unlike the other Yalies in Courtney's crowd, he has picked himself up, gone back to Yale, worked his way through by ghosting study outlines, and is now at Harvard Law School. He sternly lectures Courtney on the importance of sobering up and getting serious about things, but she is not inclined to listen until one fateful day when Janet Parker has a nasty argument with her substance-dependent father. (Indeed, virtually every character in this book would be considered an

alcoholic by current standards, but it so happens that Mr. Parker, as Pamela Moore so stringently observes, "no longer cared for the niceties of companionship or ice in his bourbon.") And then:

> [He] set down his drink and walked across the living room to her. His eyes were cold and totally without emotion. For the first time in her life, Janet was afraid of her father. She held her ground, refusing to move as he came up to her. Coldly, with the full force of his body, he slapped her . . . . He fell upon her and forced her onto the couch and lay above her as a lover might, and she was terrified. This was too strange and too strong for her, her father lying on her body in control of her . . . . As her body went limp in his arms he rose and walked over to the window. Thank God, she thought. Thank God he got up. He leaned against the window sill in shame and hatred of himself and buried his face in his hands. The intermittent and lonely sounds of the taxi horns and a train leaving Grand Central deep beneath the street rose to the window from Park Avenue. Dazed, Janet got up and ran into her room, locked both doors.

Janet puts on Stan Kenton's "Capital Punishment," goes to the window, and jumps. It is worth observing that scenes depicting father-daughter incest were uncommon during this time in American fiction, except where they could be depicted as something that happened among the picturesque and brutish lower classes. Fitzgerald's *Tender is the Night*, the most notable exception, may have been in Pamela Moore's mind when writing this scene.

Courtney reads of Janet's death in the *Times* the following morning, and goes into seclusion for weeks, refusing to speak to Anthony and Charles when they call. But, finally, it is time for her to meet Anthony for cocktails at the Plaza; to hear him out as he acknowledges that she has outgrown his act; and to proceed to Sardi's for dinner with her reconciled parents and the young, virile Cunningham. She is now ready to put in the requisite two years of college before dropping out to get hitched after he passes the bar. The tame ending was obviously tacked on to please the reviewers and pacify parents who otherwise would have been mortified with the heroine's escapades. But Pamela was not interested in repeating this formula.

V.

Moore's two novels which were never published in hardcover in America—*Diana* and *The Exile of Suzy-Q*—are her two weakest, and may be dealt with briefly. *Diana* is an ambitious book, dealing with a dozen characters and following three plot lines, and concerns a situation of considerable sociological interest: the transition of St. Mark's Place in Manhattan from a Polish and Ukrainian working-class neighborhood to a playground of New York's Beats. Unfortunately, one of the plot lines is a sappy rewrite of *Romeo and Juliet* via *West Side Story* (hence the book's U.K. title, *East Side Story*) and the other two subplots, though less sentimental, are not handled convincingly. A trio of gay men living in the same building as the title character are treated more in the fashion of the "sterile, noncreative" stereotype of the period than in the manner of *Chocolates*. The descriptive passages are overwritten and contrast unfavorably with the spare prose of Pamela's first novel.

Suzy-Q is Moore's longest and flimsiest book; its jacket copy cites *Lolita*, and like that novel *Suzy-Q* has a pubescent heroine, descriptions of the wide-open spaces of the West, and a sleazy Hollywood character or two. Pamela Moore, like Nabokov, also begins by making the reader think a comic romp is in the offing and ends by describing a homicide and the imprisonment of the heroine's would-be lover, while the girl herself, saddened and scarred, remains. The comparisons, unfortunately, end there. Moore's characters are hopelessly stereotyped, her plot jumbled and melodramatic. While the intentional humor falls flat, the serious passages, seemingly concocted by stirring together fragments of Steinbeck, Lawrence, and Graham Greene, are unintentionally ludicrous. The descriptions of horses and the landscape are occasionally well written, but such moments are rare. Both *Diana* and *Suzy-Q* conclude with ineptly handled death scenes; in Pamela Moore's final novel she moved on to the subject of spiritual death and was able to come much closer to echoing the tragic spirit of *Lolita*.

Any perceptive reviewer of *The Horsy Set* in 1963—that is, had anyone reviewed it at all—would have been obliged to point out that it had more in common, at least formally, with Françoise Sagan's books than did *Chocolates For Breakfast*. Unlike Pamela Moore's other books, *The Horsy Set* is more of a *récit* than a *roman,* a first-person narrative in which the narrator details some traumatic experience which altered his or her perception of self and world. Again the book is set in 1953, and again Moore's central figure, Brenda Palmer, née Betty Baroszy, is troubled by all the usual symptoms of incipient existentialism: Kierkegaard's "fear and trembling," Sartre's nausea, and Dr. H.S. Thompson's "fear and loathing." Although the opening pages of the book—which were no doubt the basis on which Simon & Schuster took it—faithfully echo *The Catcher In The Rye's* Lardneresque beginning, the book's tone after them more and more resembles that of Jim Thompson's most furious paperback originals; or, more precisely, a Jim Thompson who had perused Blanchot's *Les Très-Haut* and André Baillon as well as Swift and E. Howard Hunt. J.D. Salinger's Gnostic theme of the inherent iniquity of the adult world is certainly present in Moore's last book, but the glorification of the child, especially the girl-child, that suffuses *Catcher* and "A Perfect Day For Bananafish" is quite absent.

We learn that Brenda, like Moore's other heroines, has really had no childhood and never seen her father, who, according to her mother, was a bisexual Gypsy circus performer. From the time she reached her eighth birthday, Brenda has been trained under the meticulous auspices of her mother, an ex-showgirl married to an investment banker, toward the goal of making the Olympic equestrian team. As the book opens, Brenda has just gotten her only A in high school, for a senior term paper titled "Training The Horse Trains The Rider." Again the Moore heroine is dating yet another ineffectual Ivy League dropout, this one an ex-Harvard mama's boy, Larry Harfield, who's breaking into the world of off-Broadway theater by backing productions, all the while working, he assures Brenda, on a play all about her. For Brenda, this promise compensates for Larry's extracurricular sexual activity that, he insists, has been brought on by her unwillingness to shed her virginity—a determination Brenda has announced on page two. Sexuality in *The Horsy Set* is not all soft lights and gentle music as it had been in *Chocolates*; nor does it conform to the phrase, seemingly alluding to Danae's conception by Zeus—"She was open to the world, and the sun entered through her thighs"—employed in *Suzy-Q*. Moore's new metaphor for sexuality, reiterated constantly through the book, reflects considerable distaste:

> I mean there's a whole area of life that's muddy to me no matter how much I hear or read about it. So sometimes I listen to people and I don't understand them and I know they're talking from that mud; they're talking about how it feels and tastes and smells, and I get dizzy thinking I'd know just what was going on if only I took one little step and sank into that sea of mud with them, because they're all in it together.

The book's early chapters describe a group of affluent couples in Westchester County, New York, whose lives revolve around the Silver Birch Stables. The wives, like mares around a steed, all sleep with Guy, the grizzled, amoral ex-cowboy riding master, and the husbands all play it cool. Brenda's problem is that her mother isn't bothering to put up a front to her stepfather, and the latter is about to storm out and get a divorce.

As the book's narrative develops, Brenda gets into a tiff with Larry over her interest in a Lieutenant Richard Kar, a West Point cadet who, the Korean War just over, has been sent to the stable to train for the Olympic trials. Brenda and her Harvard man then go to the Richard the Lionhearted bar, a Manhattan hangout for the kind of people who populated *Chocolates*. There, she meets Patsy, to whom she takes a liking—partly because the latter "look[s] too independent to be from a cloistered school like Wellesley or Smith," partly because the two look like each other. The overtones of narcissistic lesbianism, however, do not culminate in a happy bedding as they do in so many recent novels, but in a cataclysm harsher in some ways than that in the film *Single White Female*.

At the bar, Patsy proposes that everybody go back to her place for a party. Those invited include Brenda and Larry, Brenda's best friend Chrissy, and Chrissy's date, Lieutenant Kar, who has meticulously tossed back ten shots of scotch at the bar—each one for a schoolmate killed in Korea. He's a cad, but he proceeds like the rest to Patsy's apartment, which is not furnished in standard Radcliffe Alum: It has black-and-white tile flooring, "rosy" fluorescent lights, and mirrors. This is because Patsy is a $500-a-night call girl. (The figure is still a high one nowadays, but in 1953 dollars this sum would be improbable unless Patsy's clientele consisted of King Farouk and the cream of Palm Beach and Newport.) What follows, given Patsy's fondness for giving Harvard men a $400 discount, is only logical:

> "But listen—" [Patsy's] hand now gripping my shoulder—"don't you be scared about Larry. He's an artist and a real man. He's a hundred times better man, just man, than all those guys out there. And believe me, I know."
>
> I turned to ice, staring at her sentimental eyes; I froze with a hate I couldn't control and she felt it. I didn't move but she pulled her hand off my shoulder and her face twisted.
>
> "Oh, God," she moaned.
>
> I wanted to hit her and I wanted to cry and I wanted to get out of there, and sixteen things that I should have said came to my lips but died there . . . .

In the society in which they live, Brenda and Patsy are both property, the difference being that Patsy rents herself, while Brenda is to sell herself as a life estate. They are both obliged to see each other not as people who can share a friendship, but as competitive adjuncts of Larry's whims.

What Brenda does next, less than an hour after being addressed as the "hundred-proof virgin" at the Richard the Lionhearted Bar, is to drag Larry into the call-girl's bedroom and lose her virginity—to enter the metaphorical sea of mud. And abruptly a metaphor describing another kind of sea arises as Brenda, now speaking as Betty Baroszy and addressing the last of Pamela Moore's absent fathers, says:

> Yes, [Palmer] adopted me because he's a sentimental bastard, but I didn't care, all the while I was waiting to grow up so I would find you, Father. Now I'm a woman and I'll stay with you forever, won't I, Father? Yes, never leave you, never sail backwards across the crimson sea; it's over now Father, I murdered my childhood before she could murder me, I did it Father and now you will love me forever and never shall I return across that crimson bloody sea.

Following these lines on the most disturbing of all Pamela's pages, her characters abandon the crimson sea for one ugly roll in "the mud" after another. Brenda's subsequent encounters with Larry leave her and him unsatisfied; he dismisses her as a "frigid virgin." Brenda's mother counsels marriage. Lieutenant Kar waits in the wings, and for Brenda's eighteenth birthday takes her back to the Lionhearted bar, where Larry and Patsy are dallying. In the best tradition of the American military, the officer then: a) gets into a shouting match with Larry; b) falsely asserts that he has slept with Brenda; c) slugs Larry; d) takes Brenda back to the stable and, in the mud, "shows" her what a "real man" is "all about." The book ends with Guy the riding-master fleeing Westchester County, the "horsy set" screaming each other's most gossiped-over "secrets," Brenda ditching her riding career, and Lieutenant Kar sabotaging his last ride so that the two of them can go off to a base in Germany. The acid tone Moore takes might indicate that, like *Chocolates*, this ending is not to be read seriously, but still her character is unable to conceive of life apart from being a component of a man's life.

Had Pamela lived and continued writing, perhaps she would ultimately have proven incapable of serious literature and would have finished her career composing smart but schlocky bestsellers, stylish counterparts of Danielle Steele and Jackie Collins. (Indeed, Rona Jaffe, whose 1957 success *The Best of Everything* was compared to *Chocolates* by reviewers, has spent forty years writing such novels). But her work frequently manifests a fairly sophisticated awareness of her society and its workings, whether satirically or melodramatically expressed, that is absent from the other three writers. This awareness gives her first and last books what lasting value they have. Moore's writing may have been polished, but still it was the work of a woman who either could not or, to some extent, was not allowed to mature as a writer, a woman desperately in need of the kind of social changes which the feminist movement brought into being over the years that followed. From a purely clinical perspective, and given *Chocolates* description of bipolar depression and how *The Horsy Set* in its most frantic pages epitomizes a classic "mixed state," it is important to remember that those years also saw the introduction of the first, rather ineffective, medications for depression. Her chronicles of an America still with us in some ways, and in others as distant as the world of Charlemagne, deserve serious critical examination and republication.

Zoned Bohemian

MIKE NEWIRTH

BEHIND these pretty, pricey streets of West Town lingers a neighborhood of dim ghosts: The grimy filigree of the Milwaukee Avenue firetraps, the cornices dated to the nineteenth century, the snaking alleys of oxblood cobbles, and the smoothworn, narrow railway tracks that disappear into brick walls. A neighborhood that for fifty years was serene in its limitations, insulated from the wealth and the speeds of the city. There was plant and factory work, cheap food in lunchrooms and bodegas, cheap rents in the helter-skelter whitewashed warrens, the dozens of large old apartment buildings that were grandly built and now wear thick skins of grime and listing fire escapes. The kids were cutups, playing ball, kicking ass, running with the Latin Kings. Every corner had its tavern that stayed open late. They had empty streets where on lazy summer nights they fixed their own cars, parts strewn on oily sheets. They had their own streets.

It was not so long ago, the late eighties, that the central intersection of Milwaukee-North-and-Damen was untraveled and desolate at night, a drab part of the city just off the Blue Line el where a few wornout cars sat on the streets, and only the cops, oldsters, and stout Polish regulars moving slowly in the lit windows of the Busy Bee testified to any neighborhood life. But by 1993 circumstances were beginning to weave a desired destination out of the old neglected neighborhood. The streets packed dense with old homes and six-flats were suddenly valuable to the local landlords and the local media hungry to catch an edge, and soon enough the hipsters and homeowners were trickling in, filling up the smoky bars: the Rainbo Club, which had always been there, and thus could claim the rarefied air and snooty staff of an established spot, and the upstart rooms like Sweet Alice and Uncle Wally's. That was the year *Billboard* anointed the neighborhood as the new nexus of cutting edge Chicago, even printed a *map* of West Town to assist the A&R sharks in searching out the next big thing, which turned out *not* to be Urge Overkill or Loud Lucy. Within a few years a consortium of Wrigleyville scene-profiteers had moved into the celebrated intersection, transforming a perfectly adequate shitkicker

bar into a noxious concert hall known as the Double
Door. And the youthful explorers, the Art Institute kids
and earnest disheveled recent grads, kept on coming,
tentatively at first, like tourists with their laminated
maps and personal security alarms, then as proud rent-
ers, until so many had arrived that the streets were
no longer lazy or empty but a rising sea of congested
boho cool.

The earnest, unquestioning nature of the crowd was
an early tip-off to the artifice of their spangly new
environs, the energies at work as flimsy as the rehab
walls of the newly subdivided shabby old apartments.
A lot of people saw that big intersection—anchored by
the opposing prows of the forebodingly deco Coyote
Building and the sleek, white-tiled Flatiron—and decided that this grimy, haphazard neighborhood was *it*,
the place for them, the destination they'd been promised. Or else a place for easy speculative profit. Until
finally, like an organic change, West Town was transformed into Wicker Park: Now the cars stack up for
blocks to pass under the el, through the same intersection, lined by the somber gray faces of galleries and
restaurants. You can't just *park* here, anymore; on Milwaukee the valets line up impassively in their orange
vests to take your keys and money.

When West Town—a neighborhood dormant for
years, torn and frayed, run into the ground—was re-
animated in the public eye, its landscape of neglected
real estate turned volatile. The space of buildings,
houses and taverns and commercial boxes and two-
flats, mutated into a liquid, as flexible as capital itself. Even now that the area is so well established in
its trendy hipness that it's really become a bit stodgy,
there are still enormous profits to be wrung out by the
brave. A developer buys a rat-trap house of brick, a
back house or old carriage house on the west edge,
facing Humboldt Park, hands off an incredible windfall, tens of thousands, to the oldster or weary Latinos
who hold it, spends ten more to renovate, adds a whirl-
pool tub and Euro-kitchen, and then sells this *deluxe
West Village on the Park condominium* for $240,000 or
so. And every piece of cheap housing that the developers gussy up is gone for good, whisked upward into
the decorous moneyed sphere, as if it were the bourgeois promise itself that the developers were construct-

Goblins' List

The following list is a menu of
proposed and completed projects that
The Goblins, a masked musical group,
provides to record labels interested in
working with them. The superiority of
this method, as opposed to the
traditional "demo tape," should be clear.
The Goblins would like to assure readers
that the List is not a joke, and that they
are serious about every single concept
listed.

Items marked with "X" are already
committed.

GOBLIN PRIDE (CD, 10" vinyl) A
positivity themed album. "Living On
Goblin Time," "C-U-T-T-L-A-S-S," "(The
Police Are) Just Doing Their Job," "Just
Be Yourself," "Special Reach," "Giant
Robot Rock'n'Roll," "Mr. Beef," "Worst
Brother Ever," "Selena," "The Goblin
Rider," "Goblin Girl." Cover art by Alex
Wald. **(X)**[1]

SUMMER IN THE HOOD (7"
vinyl) Summer EP. "Bring Back The
Summer Alive," "Holy Ride," "Giant
Robot Rock & Roll" (Hot Summer Drums
n' Bass Remix) **(X)**[2]

**G.O.K. [GOBLINS ON
KAMPUS]** (CD EP or 12" EP) A
collection of raunchy songs and blue
jokes recorded live before a raucous
college audience. Reminiscent of Snatch
and the Poontangs and Doug Clark and
the Hot Nuts albums. Features no
profanity! "Rock and Roll Hedgehog,"
"Secrets of A Married Man (Shatner
Sex)," "Panty Raid," more.

GOBLIN VS. GOBLIN (Double
7", triple gatefold cover) Each side is a

solo record actually played entirely by each individual Goblin (unlike other bands' "solo" projects, where each member conducts pick up musicians). Listeners voting for their favorite side will determine the new leader of the Goblins. "The Phantom Creeper Meal Ticket," "Gayngels," "Take It To The Hoop/Fourth and Inches/Hat Trick," "Goblin Gate" **(X)**[3]

"GAYNGELS" b/w "AVENGING GAYNGELS"12" (12" vinyl) Dance club mixes.

"CASTLE OF FREAKS" b/w "WE'RE A WINNER" (7" vinyl) Fan-club-only single. **(X)**

CHIPS, MONKS AND CHIPMUNKS (7" vinyl) Tributes to three of the Goblins' favorite artists. A cover of the Shadows of Knight's "Potato Chip", featuring a cameo by Ol' Durty Goblin on harp (Ol' Durty was in the '60s Garage band Durty Wurds), and a Monks cover comprise side A. Side B is a medley of Goblins hits played as one song, à la The Ramones in "Rock'n'Roll High School," sped up to Chipmunk voice speed.

NIGHT ROCKERS (7" vinyl) European release of Garage songs based on the career of David Hasselhoff. "Night Rocker," "Night Rider," "Night Rescue," "Night Kostabi" (instrumental). Cover art by Darren Merrinuk. **(X)**[4]

STONE AND BUN (7" or CD EP) New songs based on misheard lyrics. Includes "Dirty Gene and the Thunder Chief," "Chug-A-Lug, The Strawberry Man Is Making Me Crazy," more.

GIANT ROBOT EP (7" vinyl) "Giant Robot Rock'n'Roll," "Chic-A-Go-Go," "Creepy Porno Guy" **(X)**[5]

BIGELOW ASSORTED TEAS (7" vinyl) Acoustic coffeehouse songs based on tea flavors. "Constant Comment," "Earl Grey," "Lemon Lift," "Cinnamon Stick".

33 1/3 GOODWOODSMAN LANE (CD, LP) "Goblin Time Bomb,"

ing in the air above its foundation, out of ceiling fans and granite countertops.

THE developer is an easy figure to hate, but it can only be said in his defense that he is a man of the moment, a gelatinous creature who seeks only to expand, to fill the air. All the petulant carpings that make up the do-gooder exposés and community group blather—the notion of "community" as anything other than a buyable thing, the concept of persons displaced, the residue of history, the gone jobs of these ghost factories—this entire dusty web of ideas is simply invisible to the developer. So if we're to stoop to the comforting hypocrisy of blame, let's keep things simple and blame the yups, the buyers of the mini-lofts and pale new blockhouse condos. They're the eager participants who should know better, and it's their lust for the correctly purchased life in the city's most *now* quadrant that speeds the teardown of organic neighborhoods, and they really do deserve their portion of blame for that.

But for one who lives in Wicker Park there's no argument to be made that gentrification is anything but unstoppable, that the neighborhood's carefully fanned heat and the accompanying rain of greed could produce anything but this frantic division and degradation of the spoils. The last carousel is finally spinning in Algren's old neighborhood, as the hard-won occupations that raised this city sashay back toward the static imaginary past, down the cool lights of the expressways, out toward the endless deathland of industrial parks beyond the city's furthest edge. In the future maybe we'll all be options clerks, or run UNIX networks, piss in a cup and wear the gleaming suits of movie assassins, and away from our ten-hour office days we'll sleep, orgy, and thrive in our own crisp white boxy condos, all the luxury mini-lofts fabricated out of the ghostspace of a city gone to history.

The paradox of the Wicker Park scene is that what disappears is the very thing of authenticity that all the new arrivals are seeking; it becomes something they can only seek to emulate, both as individuals and as consumers within a larger commercial enterprise. And in that emulation is a growth as invisible as cancer, the hearty hollow boom time that's already left its cement skeleton along the main drags of a thousand suburbs, all the sad Levittowns and Winnetkas. Now each new hello-kitty swinger's retreat or daringly themed post-ethnic restaurant only hastens the collective demise; each new arrival dims by degrees the shine, the buzz, ensures that the cutting-edge Wicker Park scene can only be ephemeral, counts down toward the final disappearance of credibility, of the elusive glare of the public moment. From the travails of the landscape here it appears that money, like water, seeks its own aesthetic level: So it is that the favored gritty neighborhood becomes the shunned suburbs, freakish in its whiteness and jut-jawed macho conformity.

In the meantime the new occupants of Wicker Park have little choice but to continue emulating what's gone, what they've come here to find. What remains—what we're left with—exudes the fakey, tacked-up disappointment of a high school talent show. Hence the rise of a new caste of cliquish passivity, the professional bohemians and coffee-shop rebels who slouch among the tables at Earwax and Urbis Orbis, trying out their scowls, buying the lattes, the frappes, the wholesomely ethnicized flesh-free food, obsessing within the secret notebooks, arguing, expounding spittily upon their complicated lives, hatching the diatribes that fill the grotty fanzines; all their needs attended to by the pinch-faced students, pulling the teat of the espresso machine, over and over, a sticky eight-hour shift, cash in the register, the tip jar clinking. There is a perfume of insiderdom in the stale air of these coffee shops, a scene built on streams of gossip, news, projects, the ambition to cause some sort of stir that will embed an individual into the public mosaic, the little footnotes and momentary ripples to which urban "edge" culture has been reduced.

Traces of what's been replaced float like ghosts through the streets of the neighborhood. Near Division and Damen was the Czar Bar, a dark scuzzy rec-room-type establishment run by middle-aged Poles, where for a few good years touring bands like Unrest and Beat Happening and uneasy local stuff like Homocore found a roost, to the point where the Poles got some money and rehabbed the bar into a light, airy rec-room. But now it's shuttered. A few doors away, though, the Smoke Daddy is crowded with white people seated in tight groupings, eating tasty low-country

"Night Nurse," "Riding On My Ninja," "Crank Me," "Monkey Chow," "Piranhas," "Sump'n Frickin' Crazy," "Carmen," "Millennium," "Lucky Pierre," "Blue Don't Boogie," "This Beat Is Out of Control (bonus beats)," more.**(X)**[6]

BUHTRONICS /EMPTY ROOM FULL OF BLUES (EP) The first piece is guitarist Buh Zombie's solo journey through shifting, mutated, mangled, musical and nonmusical passageways of treated guitar. In the second piece Buh reads his stories (or fairy tales, as he calls them), over naturally altered and molested Goblins' tracks and "found" sounds and narratives.

OTHER VOICES (CD, LP) The exact same concept and album art as The Doors "Other Voices," though the death of the lead singer will be merely imagined in this case.

HEALTHY MEALTHY (7" vinyl) A health-centric EP. The A-side features "Healthy Mealthy" and "Yoga Party" and the B-side features "Goblercize," an exercise regimen record for our fans.

"GOBLIN MAMBO" b/w **"GOBLIN FOXTROT"** (78 RPM 10") This archival quality 78 RPM will feature beautiful label art and heavy vinyl. **(X)**

THE GOBLINS MODERN WEDDING ALBUM (LP, CD) This features songs for and about weddings and marriages of this era, which exist despite what the "government" defines as marriage. Songs include "Hawaiian Honeymoon" (about same sex marriage, two versions), "The Littlest Ring Bearer" (about a couple who lives for years happily out of wedlock and, after having a child, decides to get married; their own baby becomes the title character), "No Strippers, Please" (a song pleading for less degrading, more gender-neutral bachelor/bachelorette parties), "They Don't Understand" (too controversial to explain here), "Dog Wedding" (instrumental), and "Today I Marry My Friend." It will also include a special dance track designed for a gay exotic dancer to perform to at a same-sex bachelor party. **(X)**

WANT LIST (one sided, white label promo only, numbered, mono 7") Based on our song "CUTTLASS," a tune about each Goblin's most coveted, sought-after record. This will appeal to record collectors. **(X)**[7]

PURE CLASS (7" Vinyl) Beau Grumpus, the artistic Goblin, leaves his brethren at the Joke Shop with this solo work. Side A is a cover of Elvis' "Vino, Dinero y Amor", and the B-side features Beau reading a chapter from his book on etiquette.

THE GOBLINS HA HA HANUKAH COMEDY/VARIETY SPECIAL ORIGINAL SOUNDTRACK (cassette) This is a soundtrack to our holiday special. "Ha Ha Hanukah," "Turtle Soup," "Paranoid," "Anarchy In the U.K." (Goblins), "Get Your Mom Some Pie for Hanukah" (John Darnielle), "Calypso Draydel," "Prayer Over The Candles" (cast). Cover art by Heather McAdams. **(X)**[8]

GOBLIN KIDS (Cassette or CD EP, possibly a CD-ROM w/animation) Much like Muppet Babies, Little Archie or Flintstone Kids, this project presents child versions of The Goblins in a way kids (and kids at heart) will be attracted to. Tape speed manipulation and joyful Bubblegum pop sensibilities will abound.

THEY CAN'T ALL BE GEMS- The Worst Of The Goblins (13"Vinyl) This record of failed projects and live songs that were instantly dropped from the set will appear on the virtually unplayable format of untrimmed 12" vinyl, meaning that the jagged excess vinyl haloing each individual pressing will remain attached. There will be little loss to the listener who is unable to get his turntable to adapt to, among others, the losers "A-M-E-R-I-C-A," "Ground Zero," "Well Baby," and the Goblins' sour-sung,

barbecue in quiet reverence beneath the carefully framed and displayed tropes of a po' folks juke joint: sepia labels of blues 78s, quaint tinted illustrations of the Maxwell Street Market, tin signs from the ol' filling station. Near the big intersection on Damen one may dine and carouse at the Silver Cloud, one of the many places striving for the dim cultural memory of the swanky cocktail lounge, this one serving funny meatloaf platters, displaying a temptingly fragile pyramid of martini glasses, offering up a booze list dense with the precious goods, the single malts and uncommon microbrews. The Silver Cloud is a handsome space, with that lucrative aura of authenticity lent by a fine old intricate dark wood and chrome backbar; this is serendipitously due to the fact that it was until recently—and for no small time—a Mexican dancing bar, a dark unretouched alcove where the buoyant tejano music issued into the then-empty street. On Milwaukee, Club Dreamerz, an evil, grafittied concrete shell—which might have been the first place in West Town to have booked arcane rock in the eighties—exists only in mist. The shell has been awarded a new skin of wood paneling and classy chairs; now it's Nick's, where a clubby benevolence greets the visitor from Lincoln Park, Evanston, the burbs, the ones who will be most pleased by this urban-themed suburban tavern, the transplanted smoke and boisterous fellowship of home.

Because the neighborhood is so old—because the dark 1880s Lodge Hall now contains the snottymouthed coffee kiosk and the kool krazy shoe store where the discerning employees will be happy to take $40 for a Wisconsin Dells ashtray they dug up at the Salvation Army—an overlay effect can disorient anyone who has lived or traveled here before, say, the past three halcyon years. On Milwaukee Avenue one can track the gentrifying tendrils to where they peter out further south, where there's still the remaindered husks of the street's former life: El Chino Tacos, the multilingual travel agent, wholesale sneaker stores, and musty Western-wear emporiums. A few blocks more and the storefronts are boarded up, soaped over, closed up early. The street here appears jettisoned, tossed out according to some scheme of benign neglect, a cabal of city pols and landlords ensuring the developers' pickings for years to come. In the early evening there is a creepy silence along this southern section of Milwaukee Avenue—the sound of absence, of still-forming things. In the go-go Chicago nineties, wealth can take the form of land speculation on the backs of urban strugglers, and the city's longevity withers in the bright fisting gaze of the market.

The celebrated intersection, meanwhile, has become a place of public theater, as tourist-friendly as "Tony & Tina's Wedding." Each weekend day the silvery el cars up above disgorge streams of visitors, ID'd by the spiffiness of their clothes, the correctness of posture that comes from visiting a heard-about place, the race to judge it against expectations. The voyeurism is in effect at night as well, when the intersection becomes the nexus of Wicker Theme Park, a land of hearty grinning celebrants with fine clothes and monodimensional faces, hungry to believe the gilded promise of good times and chosen neighborhoods, and stumbling from bar to bar, hissing through their teeth at passing women, tonguing the black poles of primo cigars, pissing on walls and windows as they sullenly search for the car to take them home, all Hondas bearing Northwestern decals looking alike. The ongoing hedon's cotillion is good for business in Wicker, from the Rama Mart with its provisions of ritualized decadence—Miller Lite, E-Z Wides, inhalers, dice, ciggies, Gatorade, Trojans, Advil, Visine, Tums—to the Soul Kitchen, where the well-outfitted swingers of the moment prime themselves for a sexalicious evening by eating the funky food, raw oysters and froufrou'd jambalaya. The money hums like vibrators in all the tight rayon pockets, but it brings with it both the trash of trash—condoms, snack wrappers, the glitter of smashed pints—and human trash, the scam artists, bar bullies, and maybe-rapers, leering around at last call.

For residents of Wicker it is different from the tourist's mode only by degrees. The stakes are personally raised. You are now a part of the scene, one of the fluid links of acquaintance and decadence, and you must act appropriately: purchase coffee-table smut and ephemeral indie mumble; spend bubbly Saturday night hopping from Mad Bar to the Note, wowing a coterie of visiting friends (getting them to pick up the tabs),

ill-concieved foray into Doo Wop, "The Clown Is Getting Married."

(IMAGINE) FUCK THE BIBLE (EP) Though as a rule The Goblins do not curse on their records, an exception is made (in the title only, no profanity on the recording) in this case, as the Goblins address those closed-minded soldiers on the evil side of the Culture War, who would censor and control art and expression (are you listening Wal-Mart?!?). Of course, they are not saying "fuck the Bible," only to imagine it. They are asking you to think! **(X)**

MISCHIEF NIGHTS (8-Track tape) Retrospective of early Goblin songs. **(X)**[9]

GOBLEARN instructional three-sided single (7" with two separate grooves on B-side) The A-side will feature a "learn to play guitar the Goblin way"/Music Minus One lesson. The cover/book will feature tablature and the record will have all but the guitar part on it. The B-side will feature a CO-STAR dramatic scene featuring the Goblins and you! The blank spaces in the scene can be filled by the listener reading along with the script in the book as he/she hones his/her acting skills. On a separate groove will be an instructional ventriloquism lesson from Dom Nation.

CHANGE THE CHILDREN (7" vinyl, CD EP) The Goblins lead a cast of celebrity guests and tribute artists in this positive "We Are The World" type record, which wont so much raise money as raise awareness of the problems of the world.

BAD INFLUENCE (CD, LP) The Goblins play Devil's Advocate here by performing songs promoting all the "wrong" values. Songs include "Crank Me, Yank Me, Give Me Crystal Meth," "Too Skinny (There's No Such Thing As)," "Everybody's Doing It," "# I Fan" (a song that addresses the fan's place in the so called "Great Concert In The Sky" with Jimi, Janis, Kurt, etc. . . and how to get there!), "Sloth Is Boss," "Can't Drive At 55" (cover), more.

"HE Is My Rock, Will You Be My Roll?" (7" vinyl) In this solo work, bassist Dom Nation, in response to the crass commercial Christian Rock of this era, returns to the glory days of the seventies GodRock movement. Have faith . . . that this record will rock your earthly world!

subGOBLINS (7" vinyl) On one side the Goblins drop their singer to perform the H/C classics they cut their teeth on. On the flip the lead singer conducts a pick up band on a song the other Goblins rejected, "Imitation Of Life," his attempt to musically do for cinematic melodramas what The Misfits did for horror films. **(X)**

SKANILINGUS/SKINILINGUS (7" vinyl) In this project, the Goblins Ska-playing alter-egos, Skanilingus take you through a tour of historical Ska classics with their composition entitled "Hooked On Ska-nics." Get ready to skank! On the flip, the Goblins attempt to bring violence back into the scene in their Oi personas.

THE GOBLINS BOOKMOBILE (CD EP, Vinyl EP, Cassette) Musical interpretations of the world's great literature. A Cliff's Notes for the Post-MTV Generation. Includes "The Bell Jar," "Tropic Of Cancer," and a yet to be determined Turow novel. The cassette version can be marketed alongside Books On Tape.

"MAD AS HELL" b/w **"STAND UP YOU GOBLINS!"** (7" vinyl) The A-side is a musical tribute to that master of comedic mayhem, Gallagher. On the B-side, each Goblin tries his respective hand at one minute of original observational stand-up comedy material.

YE GOBLINS SEX SHOPPE (Large hole 9" vinyl) A tasteful exploration into erotic Goblins themes. "Sex Mensch," "Bicurious?," "Creepy Porno Guy (Orgasm Remix)," the title

then slouch hungover all the next day at the Friar's Grill. Or it may also happen that what you feel is a sort of indictment: that uncomfortable knowledge that something has gone wrong, that behind all the hard-priced, slickly bohemian cheer that's been tattooed up and down these old streets is a history—and even a people, a living population—that is ignored, spat on and forsaken.

The aloof yuppie hipsterism that defines Wicker Park can trace its origins to the decisions of artists and other disreputable sorts to move here around 1983, when Huey Lewis was the King of Rock and Roll, and All The Young Dudes lived in Wrigleyville and Lincoln Park and partied on the Division Street meat market strip. Today the artist archetype is West Town's equivalent of Joe Camel, a promotional image wafted over the city to help sell condominiums. The dubious contrast between old and new—between a "real" bohemia and the frat party that replaced it—may read like cheap sentiment, the gloomy boozer's trip back to his narrow town. And yet the difference here is so sharp and evident as to be undeniable. Today Wicker Park hipsterism exhorts from us only an enthusiastic apathy—the hearty cry of "I know nothing!" in the face of the blatant swindle—in return for the elusive assurances encoded in all the bought objects, the insubstantial retro gear, the puckish publications offering guides to the moment's favored cultural ironies, the focaccia, the electronica. Meantime, any notion of action or protest—to say nothing of resistance—dissolves in favor of shallow self-articulation. The stations of this theme park are manned by all the in-crowd, the hipsterists, whose contempt for those they attend and serve oozes out as they giggle and confer over their after-parties and connections and secret schemes.

The hipsterists share a lot with the capitalists—in particular the notion of getting in early, being the first on board a cultural referent like a good growth stock. Raw ambition animates much of the local culture in its race toward the ever-vanishing "edge," a culture whose products—pop-cult worshipping zines, arcanely abrasive rock, Dayglo T&A artwork, poetry slams at the sandwich shop—are almost impossible to regard as anything more than grease in the mechanisms of self-promotion. When the dust settles in two years or so, a lucky handful of the hipsterists will have extruded careers, signifiers, lucre, from the co-opted chaos of their Wicker efforts; others will retreat to the cushioned disappointment of boozy recall within a duller life, to grousing over how close they came. Only the landscape will remain constant as it accommodates this discourse, the frantic assertion of competitive difference, underwritten and supported by legions of followers who are as set in their ways as any North Shore Republican.

The cops and bankers who desultorily cruise the intersection can sleep restfully, knowing 1968 will never return to Chicago. For all the irksome young bohemians so urgent in their visibility, it's unlikely that this place will ever see many stabs at actual resistance—no grimy Loisaida squatters at work in Wicker, no one left to terrorize the landlords—nor are there even many echoes of the disgruntled punk rock scene that flourished in Chicago in the eighties, the lacerating sounds of Bloodsport, Naked Raygun, Effigies, Big Black, along with the stirring community fostered by the half-populated clubs Batteries and Dreamerz—something almost unknown to the Wickerites, who were then in their Rob Lowe-on-Div-Street incarnation.

So the scrabbling bohemians set the tone, and provide the diverting amusements in the glittering galleries and shops, but it is the handsome, self-assured, well-employed earners who literally own this place. The last laugh of gentrification is—surprise!—enjoyed by its natural constituency, the Midwestern strivers who've done so well since the '91 recession, and who have tried so hard to create a permanence for themselves by buying into the sanctioned, praised urban space of a city they never before knew—West Town, Logan Square, the "lofts" of the South Loop—that you can no longer see the frantic pace of land speculation here, only sense it in the absurd muggings of the costs, the public discourse of money, in sums probably you and I—certainly the people who lived here for thirty or so years—cannot really conceive of pulling together.

Most of the new constructions in Wicker are naked blockhouses of brick and cement, featuring one significant feature of ornament: an enormous central window, revealing the living room and more, the home's

track and more. Though it was not originally intended, it has been pointed out by the production designer that this record's large hole and suggestive label art may cause some male fans to mistake this for a functional "marital aid."

Compilation tracks: "Bread and Butter," "I'm Gonna Make You Mine," "Mr. Beefjangles," "My Mother The Car"**(X)**, "Lucky Star"**(X)**, "Oh How To Do Now,"**(X)** "Bull Run" **(X)**.

The Goblins are interested in working in these formats: Picture disc, reel to reel, 5" vinyl, 6" vinyl, 8" vinyl, 9" vinyl, 11" vinyl, CD3, longbox CD, pop up gatefold 7", comic book and record set with beeps, backward-groove record, Scratch-and-Sniff sleeve, You-Build-It perforated model or mobile kit sleeve.

1. Available now, on CD from Atavistic/Truckstop (P.O. Box 578266, Chicago, IL 60657) and on vinyl from Mind Of A Child (P.O. Box 1586, Findlay, OH 45839)

2. Available now from Won't Go Flat Records (P.O. Box 379463, Chicago, IL 60637)

3. Available now from Mind Of A Child

4. Available soon from Pure Vinyl (c/o Gerhard Fluch, Sandgasse 8b a-4020, Linz, Austria)

5. Available now from Won't Go Flat.

6. Available soon from Atavistic/Truckstop

7. Available soon, in very limited quantity, from Trixie (P.O. Box 379373, Chicago, IL 60637)

8. Available now from Shrimper (P.O. Box 1837, Upland, CA 91785-1837)

9. Available now from Underdog (2201 N. Rockwell, Chicago, IL 60647)

The Goblins can be contacted at 1507 E. 53rd St. #617 Chicago, IL 60615.

notion of public space made literal. The big window allows the occupying yuppie to display not just his skinned-looking house, but every last thing he's purchased to complete the urban living experiment, the brave way he's set out to live.

This sort of ostentation is already routine at Con Fusion, one of this year's most chic Chicago restaurants, where the well-dressed and supercilious line up to contemplate an abstruse, variegated cuisine—a beef in port sauce here, some star anise there, edible flowers atop the peppercorn ice cream. The real draw of Con Fusion lies in a certain triumph of design: The restaurant is a large space where nearly every component is the palest white, with furniture of transparent hard plastic, so that the inevitable floor-to-roof windows facing Damen create for those on the street an aquarium of the baroque spending rituals of trendy dining.

The management is known to stock the window tables with whatever celebrities drop by—Marilyn Miglin, Liz Phair—or failing that, to sift out the glossiest among the arriving guests, the tallest, slimmest women, the bejeweled men, just as the red-vested attendants have been ordered to stack up the finest rides—the sterile Mercedes, the occasional Ferrari—on the narrow slice of street outside. It is impressive to walk past Con Fusion late at night and view this bright scene, the display of the well-heeled and their personal assets, faces frozen above the small helpings of fussily arranged food. The sad austerity of the Con Fusion scene sets it apart from the garden-variety vulgarity of Wicker Park consumption: Watching the patrons squint in vain at the long procession of designer novelty, always waiting for satisfaction, is like looking into a specimen case of the future and seeing how vulnerable life is, even in the bright protected enclosures of the rich.

And there's also that possible future that nobody here wants to talk about, the notion of the pendulum swinging back, that what we've done here will in the end get done to us. A collapse in the housing market, a Midwest recession, a stock market crash, or urban unrest when the thousands of West Side disenfranchised come around at last to demand their due—each could shred the safe happy bubble we now inhabit in so many of the colonized neighborhoods of this city. Or, if this notion of urban meltdown seems

Hunter Kennedy

uncomfortably fantastic here in the autumn of surging productivity, consider instead the ending that is already rushing to meet us, the expiration date, the self-destruct. Already the seams are showing in Wicker Park, as each weekend the streets clog with the loud well-dressed celebrants in their gleaming new cars and loud posses, crowding the streets, woozy with drink, uncertain where to go next, coming unhappily upon the inescapable conclusion that the bars and lounges and supper spots in the end are pretty much the same, that there's no place left to go here that will startle or shake them. It seems only a matter of time before Wicker is mostly known for its smog-belching hordes of sport utilities, its black-hole real estate loss-leaders, its stogie-huffing sports-bar boozers and uptight white restaurant patrons. "Wicker Park? That's, like, so 1995!" It is a tantalizing dream, West Town reduced again to its old place, the lofts burnt out, fire-sale real estate signs glutting streets suddenly free of Range Rovers, once again quiet, ignored.

H ERE at the end of the century, a certain notion of "artistic community" has become one of our most hallowed social institutions. Maybe it's an ideal that once made some sort of obvious and clearly defined sense, in those sepia garrets where Alice B. prepared the naughty brownies; and maybe somewhere it does still, like amongst the polite and enthusiastic chosen who appear each summer at Breadloaf, or the sullen polyester-sheathed chosen who grind

away in the crowded Art Institute workshops. But the degree to which this cherished ideal has become a public hallucination is the real story of the siege of Wicker Park. After all, it took fifty years for the Greenwich Village of John Reed, Max Eastman, and John Sloane to become the "scene" of Warhol, *The Basketball Diaries*, heroin, and the tourist-squeeze routine of shitty meals, head shops, and bad clubs it is today. The strange and frightening fact about Wicker is that the region's lamination took only five years or so—five years for the bohemian simulacrum to reproduce itself on the rubble of what was real. And the thread has a ways to play out still, into the sad finale in which everyone will see past the bright lights and new flashy signs of the Milwaukee Avenue pleasure strip, and the great sheepish exodus that will follow: the big ugly hangover of unadorned realization which awaits.

Youth these days consists of the accumulation of money and memory, ensuring that every last frantic experience counts toward some ultimate accumulation, some reminiscence to treasure far out in the suburbs when the city at last is left behind. This is why in all the neighborhoods like Wicker Park these days the young employeds hurry home off the evening el, clutching their Coach bags and cell phones, the tight toes of their shoes tap-tapping. And in the safety of apartments they shed their constrictive disguises and reappear, no longer drones but dashing and sly, in their tight, gaudy, ill-fitting, carefully coordinated and expensive designer swinger suits of polyester, stretch, and pleather, hurrying *back*, toward the intersection, past the crackhead panhandlers who soon enough will be gone, toward the bright spangly nightclubs and bars. This is the time of celebration, of the solemn ironic party, and they walk down the dark sidewalks with great haste, the employed rebels with their carefully trimmed VanDykes, the career gals in their important nostalgic shoes, this is *their* time, pausing to raise their Zippos to their European smokes, yearning for the walls of their nightclubs, the carefully resurrected cocktail lounges crammed with martinis and cigars, tropes of youth and money ferried to them in the invisible hands of servers, camaraderie and good fellowship trailing gin vapors off the triangular heads of the frosted glasses. On these evening streets they may brush past occasional former inhabitants of their neighborhood, the old codgers who still live in set-aside low-income housing on Damen, solid grammas with grocery carts and walkers, crooked-eyed geezers who also wear too-tight synthetics, who might actually dimly recall gambling against Nelson Algren, who knew this city when it was really potent, cruising in their very slow way up the sidewalk, back to their small rooms, hurrying to get out of the way.